Aurea Vidyā Collection*

———————— 16 ————————

* For a complete list of Titles, see page 191.

BEYOND DOUBT

Published by Aurea Vidyā in 2013
39 West 88th Street, New York, N.Y.
www.vidya-ashramvidyaorder.org

This book was originally published in Italian as
Raphael, *Di là dal Dubbio, Accostamenti alla Non-dualità*
by Edizioni Āśram Vidyā, Rome, Italy. 1982.

©Āśram Vidyā 1979
 Second Edition 2001
 English Translation ©Āśram Vidyā 2013

Printed and bound by Lightning Source Inc. at locations in the
U.S.A. and in the U.K., as shown on the last page.

The revenues from the sale of this book, for which there are no
copyright obligations, will be used for reprints.

ISBN 978-1-931406-16-1

Library of Congress Control Number: 2013909891

On the cover: Caravaggio: *Narcissus*. Rome, Galleria Nazionale
d'Arte Antica in Palazzo Barberini.

Raphael
(Āśram Vidyā Order)

BEYOND DOUBT

Approaches to Non-duality

AUREA VIDYĀ

The search for the absolute is the noblest and most worth while task of science because everything that is relative presupposes something that is absolute and is meaningful only when juxtaposed to something absolute.

Max Planck

TABLE OF CONTENTS

Presentation   11

Sensorial Materialism   19
The Philosophy of Being   43
Karma, Sādhanā and Culturalism   55
Points of View and Erudition   63
Original Sin and Christianity   73
Transformation of Consciousness and Techniques   81
Name, Form and Vāsanās   91
Vibrating Life   107
Asparśavāda   121
Post Mortem and Bardo Thötröl   133
Ahaṁkāra   155
Separation   163
Ākāśa and Meditation   169
Dying to Oneself   173

Index   179
Raphael: Unity of Tradition   185

PRESENTATION

Beyond Doubt is a work in which Raphael again engages in a dialogue that springs from a need for inquiry. On one side of the dialogue, we see a wandering in the shadow of insecurity and loss, and on the other, a firm position of consciousness of *Advaita* Knowledge (Non-duality). This Knowledge is devoid of opposition and is founded on a comprehension that accepts others as they are. It is therefore able to give to each, without any forcing, what the situation of consciousness requires in that very moment.

The person initiating the dialogue presents a rigidly materialistic faith based on sensorial perception and experience. He is an "atheist" who not only does not believe in God because he cannot find proof of His existence, but also does not believe in anything at all. Raphael does not reply immediately to the question presented, but rather asks other appropriate, precise and stringent questions, bringing the questioner to the point of entangling himself in contradictory statements. Meanwhile, in a Socratic way, Raphael guides him into acquiring an increasingly deeper comprehension of his thinking and discovering truth on his own.

At first, although he is still anchored to empirical and sensorial reality and limited by such a vision, the questioner is forced to admit the existence of an intelligence-energy; but soon afterwards, like a child who recovers a discarded toy because he is still attracted to it, he again obstinately insists that "all is matter," retreating into simplistic positions such as "I believe what I see and perceive."

But to believe in matter that changes while it is observed, that because of its fluidity is not a basis for valid, real and constant knowledge, makes the individual unhappy and anguished. How could he be otherwise? He identifies with appearances (*māyā*), with movement, with becoming, and with that which crumbles between his fingers and nullifies his efforts to build something solid, secure and trustworthy. The human being seeks and wants completeness. He wants to find himself. But he is incapable of seeing beyond the narrow confines of his egoic individuality, which obligates him to search for himself in external data, in themselves transitory and incomplete. Until he opens himself up to universal values and seeks Fullness in the depths of his own being, he will be tormented by desire and dissatisfaction.

Raphael is very present to the sufferings of this man who is unable to escape the restrictions of his own immaturity. Full of love, he points out the two pathways that lie before us: the philosophy of becoming and the Philosophy of Being. The former views man exclusively as a psychophysical compound stimulated by indefinite desires; the latter sees man in his entirety, in a relationship of Harmony with the cosmos. One on the former path requires sensorial satisfaction to quench his desires, while one on the latter seeks inner peace, an accord with all of creation and Beatitude. The aim is the same: attainment of one's own well-being. But the philosophy of becoming, source only of dissatisfaction and pain, leads the individual to look for the good in external objects—whether power, wealth, success or the products of technology—which can never satisfy his thirst for well-being and only lead to increasing wants. The Philosophy of Being, on the other hand, guides the being inward, where, freed from all external bonds, he can find Completeness.

The being bound by the philosophy of becoming is conditioned by many factors. He is held in bondage by his own mind, by the collective unconscious, by false notions and by the heap of superimpositions he himself has created. He is bound by concepts of time and space, by dualism of cause and effect, by a culture of notions typical of the world of becoming and by remorse. These useless crystallizations of the past must be overcome.

Only one who has integrated all polarity is free from all this. He is Silence and law unto himself. The Author, who "sees" man as truly free, addresses the topics that are the cause of so much doubt. He illuminates interlocutors with the light of his knowledge, Knowledge with a capital K, based on imperishable, universal principles of which He makes a continuous loving gift to the readers and to those who know how to receive it. This gift of love is the means by which Raphael conducts the being from doubt into certainty of being pure Consciousness, so that it will be easier for the being to find and reintegrate himself into Being, into *That*. This is Love without words, a sacrifice. It is an offering of one's own *pax profunda*, one's own Silence, to those on the way of *Asparśavāda* (the path without support) who are not yet able to ascend on their own.

The Master's gift, though, is not sufficient to make of the disciple a realized being: the disciple's active participation is also necessary. A life-giving ray of sunlight is not sufficient to cause the seed, sown in the protective bosom of the earth, to sprout. Just as the seed must capture that light, absorb it and avail of it for its own blossoming, so must the disciple learn to use what the Master places at his disposal to transform his consciousness. He will therefore have to live the doctrine he is taught, abandon himself to the Master's guidance and use techniques of recalling—or, rather, reawakening through Platonic "reminiscence"—all that pre-exists inside him. These are the means and supports appropriate for the type of path he follows and for the position his consciousness has attained—of which there will be no further need once the axiom "You are *That*" of the *Upaniṣads* is realized. But up until that moment, how necessary the Master is! Did Raphael even have one? This is a legitimate question one might well ask. The answer is not what one would wish, a precise indication with a name, but it is one that gives us much to meditate upon. It is the individual, says Raphael, who is unable to go beyond personification, always seeking it, forgetting that "*Brahman* may reveal Himself in limitless ways." It is necessary to reflect upon these words, which might indicate an exceptional intervention, of a type not customary to us, in the spiritual life of this Knower.

The many topics treated in this book are of such interest that as a whole they constitute nourishment from which anyone can satisfy the needs of his own intellect, culture and consciousness. As opposed to Self-Knowledge, there is mention of ego-ignorance—an ego that fears for its own survival and that sees the risk of death in silence and non-motion. The topic of sex is raised, along with how it should be released from past crystallizations, from conceptualizations of the analytical mind (*manas*) and from subconscious influences. Only then can sex return to the simple, joyful expression of sacred ritual enjoyed before it was debased to the level of physical gratification. When sex is mechanical habit anchored in grossness, it no longer experiences the beauty of freedom and Harmony, "*līlā*, innocent play like the flight of a swallow," because it carries the maculations that are typical of life today.

We have here the first reference to Harmony, the nucleus around which "Vibrant Life," one of the most beautiful and original chapters of this book, unfolds. Here all is music, tone, waves, a symphony of notes, rhythms and chords, which give the reader a harmonious vision of the life he seeks. He might hope to have senses subtle enough to awaken to the musical interrelations flowing among all creatures, to witness the cosmic concert that soars in luminous sounds from all spheres. But his limited receptive powers may prevent him from attuning himself to this euphonic universe. He might only perceive some of its peripherial notes and be barred from penetrating the wondrous mystery of a composition that unites in a stupendous single chord the vibrations of every being and every created thing.

This marvellous ascending musical scale includes all the living kingdoms man can enter into as a "musical demiurge." If he educates his "string of Consciousness," resounding harmonies will cancel pain, strife and opposition.

In this work, too, Raphael not only makes the entity responsible, but he goes much further: he sweeps him out of passive resignation, renders him active in the face of events and involves him in his own *transformation*. If the entity is sufficiently receptive to the teaching, Jesus will not have taught the value of Love in vain, Buddha will not have warned against the dangers of desire in vain and Śaṅkara will not have tried to help us distinguish between the "snake" and the "rope" in vain. Raising the tone value of one's harmonic expression (rather than increasing its volume to the point of saturation and destruction, as usually happens) is the way to improve the quality of humanity, and save it.

This chapter is so fascinating we might wish never to be torn away from it, especially because we sense that it is not a mere intellectual effort on Raphael's part, but a gift He is offering to us of experiences he has personally lived. In certain especially significant and stimulating moments, we seem to be able to enter the experience with Him, to listen and comprehend. If we were to meditate deeply upon his words, all this could one day become a reality for us, enabling us to tune together individual and universal cosmic harmony.

Spiritual writings provide an immense constructive boon. They propose theories and practice woven in truth. They arouse interiorization in the attentive, qualified reader and, more often than not, awaken latent aspirations that lead to important existential choices. An Author who gives the benefit of experienced truth to his works is a "Master of Life," a guide who brings us to a certainty beyond doubt. For this reason, when Raphael addresses the topic of *post mortem*, he does not limit himself. He explains parts of the *Bardo* that satisfy the curiosity of man about the most important event of his life after birth. He dispels the anxieties of anguished and confused egos concerning the question "what will happen after death?" But, beyond this, he indicates to us the path of realization.

By finding correspondences between expressions and concepts typical of Tibetan tradition and those of our Western tradition, Raphael presents the *Bardo* in a form that makes it accessible and valid to us. While exposition of the sequences that characterize the process of death is extremely interesting, even more important are the conclusions and considerations Raphael draws. They give us grounds for deep reflection and, above all, act as stimuli for appropriate action.

If during our incarnation we do not stabilize ourselves at the center point, if we do not learn to face all the events of becoming with detachment, we will not be able to do so afterwards. This is why Raphael says, "The *Bardo Thötröl* is not a teaching for the dead, but for the living." We need it now, in this life, because if we do not destroy our "psychological monsters" during our lifetime, they will assail us in the afterlife, drag us down again and lead us inevitably back to *saṁsāra*. What remains of the unsolved in us—unresolved seeds, desires, thirst for assertion—will seek a space, a possibility to manifest itself, to bring to completion what has remained pending. Inexorably, the unsolved will push us back into another incarnation, toward pain and suffering.

Raphael's downplaying of death (considered nonexistent if seen as transformation) is of the utmost timeliness because it urges the individual to reflect upon *his own* death. It is human nature to think about death, but of course generally with respect to other people and rarely ourselves, as if we were immune from this law. And to think that it would be granted to man, if he only so desired, to vanquish death by experiencing the events of dying in perfect awareness.

To achieve such an aim, it would be sufficient to carry out what Raphael expounds in the final pages of this work, which sum up in a single vision what he has illustrated with great clarity throughout the book.

Here he finds, at last, an interlocutor who, instead of asking him questions, offers him a description of his state of consciousness. He is Witness who, outside and beyond the movement of becoming, observes all with unruffled detachment. From the height and solitude of a "divine indifference," he sees the disorder, confusion, anguish and struggles that mankind has superimposed on all kingdoms of life: altered minerals, polluted waters, plants falling ill, animals deprived of elements essential to their survival. We are responsible for the disasters and, because of our discordant desires, continue to disharmonize the cycle of life. What can this Witness do but shift his gaze from that chaos and raise it up to the spheres that still respect interplanetary order, where harmony resounds, flooding space. And await the dissolution of the vehicles that still hold his Self in the reign of becoming, from which he is already detached. The slow death of materiality, though depriving him each day of something, nevertheless compensates him by preparing him for ultimate Liberty.

We must aspire towards this Liberty. Raphael, through the teachings he offers in this book, accompanies us up to this point. Here, beyond all indecision, with certainty-faith in our eternity, we may gather, reflect and meditate upon his most important points, which strike effective and penetrating notes while maintaining that sobriety and composure typical of Raphael.

This is another gift that Raphael offers men to bring them "beyond doubt," beyond restlessness and uncertainty to where there is no more suffering, but Certainty and Beatitude.

Marina Zannelli

SENSORIAL MATERIALISM

Questioner - I am an atheist, and I also think that it is sufficient to experience whatever life may offer. I firmly believe in my sensory experience and cannot imagine spheres that I cannot perceive...

Raphael - Sorry if I interrupt you, but what do you mean by an atheist?

— (same questioner) That I do not believe in any God.

R - Do you believe in the sun, in plants, in animals? You should be able to see these things with your physical eyes.

— Yes, of course. How could I but see them?

R - Let us say, therefore, that you believe in nature.

— I believe in life and in the experience I live through the senses.

R - It is the same thing: you believe in life-nature, and you cannot accept all that does not belong to nature.

— That is so. I do not worry about tomorrow or about possible other worlds. I believe in the life that I am experiencing, even if I do feel some kind of metaphysical curiosity.

R - As we were saying before, you believe in life-nature; therefore, you believe in something. I do not think that you refuse to believe in your own existence.

— I am not a nihilist; I am an atheist. It is not the same thing.

R - And who is it that believes in life-nature?

— It is I who do. My person, my mind and my consciousness do.

R - Therefore, there an ego-person who thinks, believes and interprets, is there not? Is there not also a consciousness?

— Yes, of course.

R - And is this ego-consciousness an integral part of nature or is it outside of or above nature?

— After death I do not believe that any aspect of me will survive.

R - Therefore, it is inherent to nature itself. Since you have mentioned death, is the ego relative, contingent and mortal?

— Yes, everything in nature dies.

R - If the ego is mortal, contingent and relative, how can you make absolute statements? A relative cannot speak of anything except relativity. Do you not agree?

— I cannot accept what I cannot perceive and cannot see.

R - There are many things that we cannot perceive and cannot see, and yet according to science they exist. If we were to accept only what the senses refer to us, we would certainly narrow our knowledge of nature considerably.

Why then are you so absolute in considering your eyes and other senses as the only instruments of observation? Could you not consider the working hypothesis of the extrasensory?

— I believe that what you call the soul, the spirit, *ātman*, etc., is nothing but nature.

R - We have already said that all is nature, including the ego that questions and interrogates itself; but it is a limited, contingent and mortal ego, is that not so?

— I believe that upon its death my ego-body will be turned into dust and simply nourish the plants.

R - So you believe in metempsychosis, do you?

— No, I do not believe in the transmigration of the soul.

R - But you believe in a body that transmigrates, and that is the same. It transmigrates into the sod of earth; it is transformed into chemical products.

— But it does not keep its memory and its mind, because these disappear completely. The mind is a compound of cells.

R - Certainly whatever is born disappears. Reason posits it, experience confirms it.
I presume you believe that nature is guided by intelligence. I do not wish to think that you believe in chance.

— Yes, I believe in an intelligent nature.

R - Certainly. Otherwise we would be obliged to attribute to chance the prerogative of intelligence, which in fact would be the very same thing.
Some believe that chance creates; others believe that it is intelligence that does so. However, here we are merely upon the plane of names. Therefore, intelligence permeates nature, does it not?

— Yes, I have no doubts about this. Otherwise I would have to hold that I too am an unintelligent animal, which is unacceptable. It is said that nature is governed by laws, which means that it is governed by intelligent action.

R - And is this intelligence innate to life itself, or is it an Entity in its own right, capable of guiding life-nature?

— This would lead us to conceive of a divinity.

R - Let's say, therefore, that intelligence is consubstantial to nature-life; this contains within itself the quality of intelligence. In other words, we are expressing a simple pantheism, and you are not the only one to think in these terms.

— Yes, but everything is merely matter.

R - And as matter dissolves into energy, we can say that all is intelligent energy. Do you not agree?

— Yes, I do.

R - I presume that this intelligent energy was born of itself; otherwise we would have to accept the existence of some other datum.

— It cannot be otherwise. Life has no other cause but life itself.

R - Seeing that all energy expresses itself in terms of polarity (positive-negative, etc.), I also presume, naturally on the basis of your point of view, that polarity is innate to life.

— Yes. It is life itself that manifests itself in polar and dualistic terms.

R - Are the two vital poles always such, or do they too transform themselves into some other kind of unifying energy?

— I do not comprehend what you mean. Can you explain what you mean?

R - For you, is duality coeternal, or does it resolve itself at some particular point? Do psyche and matter always remain separate poles, or do they resolve themselves at some point into a synthesis of the two? Or better still, did all the multiform matter that exists stem from a single and non-multiple energy?

— I have never faced this particular problem.

R - Are you a dualist or a monist?

— Do not speak to me in theological terms.

R - They are not really theological terms.

— I tend toward monism.

R - Therefore, mind and matter, quality and quantity, and all other possible dualisms dissolve into the one and undifferentiated energy, is that so?

— I think so.

R - So in the beginning we have undifferentiated energy, which gradually gave birth to the multiplicity of things. I am sorry you did not go into the question in depth because that way our dialogue would certainly have been more fruitful.

— You create many problems for me that perhaps have no real reason to exist.

R - It is the mind, alas, that creates certain problems, and it cannot help but do so.

— But did I not hear in our conversations that the mind would do well to remain silent?

R - Certainly. In this case, it should be silent, even when stating that all is nature. Do you not agree? Shouldn't the mind, then, avoid making absolute statements in the first place if it wants to be silent?

— You see, it may be that I have the inclination not to believe in anything.

R - Which means that you still believe in something. Nothing is a non-existent mental concept, like the horns of the hare. On the other hand, with your statements, you simply create more problems. So, in your proposition we have two data: "I" and "nothing"; to what does that nothing refer? To the sun, to plants, to the earth? Before, you said you believed in these things. If you did not believe in them, then we would have to agree that you believe only in your own "I," which would simply be an irrational solipsism. If only you exist, how can you ask me questions if I do not exist and am not?

— I return to my original statement, and that is: I believe in what I see and perceive. Perhaps this idea is simpler, even if it is less philosophical.

R - I do not want to oppose your thesis; I simply wish to verify whether it is possible to demonstrate your statement and whether it is possible to formulate it in terms of absoluteness. I would like to verify with you whether an exclusively sensory kind of knowledge can be considered valid. Are the eyes that see and the cells that perceive absolute?

— These things, no. But the mind can be considered absolute.

R - Then there is something in us that is absolute, is there not, which remains even after our eyes and all the rest have been transformed? But did you not say before that everything is perishable?

— Yes, it was my friend who suggested to me that the mind might be absolute.

R - However, if the mind is relative, how can it postulate absolute statements? In what way can it experience totality?

— You give me the impression that we are creating a vicious circle from which it is impossible to emerge.

R - In any case, can you put up with me and accept me?

— If I am here, it means not only that I accept you, but that I would like to believe in something above and beyond matter. Fundamentally, I feel deeply dissatisfied with life.

R - This acceptance is rational, fruitful and beautiful. I too accept you and have no intention of convincing you to believe in something that is, as you say, above and beyond matter. In universal life there are numerous theses, many beliefs and various directions or pathways along which to travel; and at the same time, the most beautiful and intelligent thing is precisely learning to accept and comprehend each other. Real ignorance does not mean following a path that is different from others, but means trying to force, oblige and overpower those who do not choose our path, those who see things differently from us.

We can love each other and live side by side, if life requires it, in the name of the intelligence and freedom that are consubstantial to nature itself. Do you not agree?

— I deeply agree with what you say. I can state that I am a liberal materialist, just as sincerely as I can state that you are a liberal spiritualist.

R - Allow me, however, to conclude by saying that as long as we state that "all is matter" or "all is spirit," we operate within the sphere of one-sidedness, opposition and dualism. When we learn to emerge from the realm of "yes" and "no," we shall have reached Unity and real, authentic Liberty.

Q - I should like to return to one of your considerations. Is *Brahman* denial or affirmation?

R - *Brahman*, or pure Being, can be neither denied nor affirmed.

— Then *Brahman* must be emptiness, must it not?

R - What you say also belongs to the world of concepts.
All possible forms of dualism are born *after* the One-
without-a-second, and if one wishes to realize the One-
without-a-second, one must transcend all duality, including
denial and affirmation.

— But how can I refuse *māyā* if it was created by
God? By refusing to recognize *māyā,* am I not opposing
God? Or, worse still, am I not denying God?

If God chose to manifest himself in such a way, he
probably had a good reason for doing so. Therefore, I
cannot refuse *māyā.* If life is what it is, why should I
refuse it?

R - First of all, it is necessary to point out one thing:
in this world there is nothing to accept or refuse; one
must simply comprehend oneself and comprehend. Therefore *māyā* cannot be either accepted or denied, but only
comprehended.[1] We can say: reality should be comprehended, and it makes sense and has a value insofar as
it is comprehended. When you say that you wish to live
"life as it is," are you sure that you are living the real
life, or are you experiencing something that is not real?
You should not rush to the conclusion that a datum is
real just because your five senses enable you to perceive
it. Because of the law of refraction, you may see two

---

[1] See also the chapter "Māyā: Apparent Movement," in Raphael,
*Tat tvam asi (That thou art): The Path of Fire according to the
Asparśavāda* (New York: Aurea Vidyā, 2002).

moons instead of one, you may see a mirage where there is dry desert, or you may have a dream full of excitement and movement when in fact you are resting and still, and so on. So, in what manner can you live these things and consider them real, just as they are? You may choose to do so, but our problem is to comprehend whether what we have experienced or perceived is real and constant.

It is often said that we must accept what we have before us, live this existence as it is, suffer and accept suffering, act, take part in politics, set up a family and serve humanity, etc. But our task is not that of accepting or refusing these things in an a priori way, but rather that of understanding whether these things correspond or not to real and absolute values. As you can see, our problem is quite different.

It is inevitable that we abandon attraction-repulsion sentimentality if we wish to base our investigation upon sound and fruitful premises. It is not, therefore, a question of accepting or refusing God, or of propounding a philosophy that makes itself dependent a priori upon a qualified and projected Entity. It is our task, on the contrary, to discover in all human and superhuman factors, in all our anxieties, in all our joy and in all our suffering, the absolute Constant or the unchanging Reality.

Q - With this view, we must recognize the fact that all is relative, and therefore we must refuse all that surrounds us. What is left to me—suicide?

R - Not all can be relative, because if it were, that would mean upholding absolute relativism, which is a contradiction in terms.

If there is a relative, there must also be an absolute because, whatever they say, being relative means *dependence*.
As I said before, it is not a question of accepting
or refusing; it is a question of comprehending what we
perceive, live and experience. I beg you not to go back
to this issue.

Q - But could we not live this relative without opposing it? Is the relative really fatal?

R - The relative is not fatal as such, but what may
prove to be enchaining is our *response* to the relative. A
phenomenon is a phenomenon, but if we approach it in the
wrong way, it can create a good deal of trouble for us.

Q - Since the relative is not simply nothing, can we
not avail of it as a field in which to live and experiment?
If it is not simply nothing, it must have some value.

R - This is a point well worth considering. *Advaita
Vedānta* and *Asparśayoga* do not consider the world of
names and forms simple nothingness, like the horns of the
hare or the child of a barren woman; but they attribute
to that world only a certain *degree of truth*, a degree that
may prove to be insignificant, negligible and of only the
slightest importance when compared to another degree of
truth.[1] Sticking to strictly scientific terminology, let us say

---

[1] For an in-depth review of the theme, refer to the chapters
"Ajātivāda and Asparśavāda" and "Advaita Vedānta," in Raphael, *The
Pathway of Non-duality: Advaitavāda* (Delhi: Motilal Banarsidass,
1992).

that there are different systems of coordinates that may all possess a *relative* value of their own, which when compared to others may prove to have no value, not even a relative one. Sometimes two systems of coordinates not only contradict but annul each other. For example, dawn and sunset are truths to terrestrials, but to a hypothetical extraterrestrial, dawn and sunset are non-realities. Besides, the good-evil that we perceive within our own set of coordinates may not even exist within another set, a fact that is asserted by the Knowers. Now, all possible systems of coordinates represent non-realities for the absolute *Brahman*; in It they dissolve themselves.

— There is, however, a strong desire to live in this relative world.

R - It is not a question of attraction-repulsion, of pleasure-pain; it is a question of knowing whether there is any sense in living and experiencing this pleasure-pain, whether it has any absolute validity, or whether it represents a prison from which we must learn to escape. This is the problem.

I see that many—that is, the majority—in order to continue in this pleasure-pain, invent sophisticated philosophies (some even of a spiritual nature), but, I insist, the problem for the serious researcher is that of knowing whether this experience of life "as it is" has a real-absolute foundation.

Reality cannot be interpreted in terms of pleasure-pain, of attraction-repulsion. Emotions do not convey the real, but rather simple *representations*, opinions and projections.

Here we are looking for the absolute Constant, and if we wish to seek it and reveal it, we must go above and beyond opinions, pleasure-pain and all regret whatsoever at abandoning what we like or what we have identified with in a sentimental and intellectual way.[1]

Q - I am, as they say, full of life and would like to enjoy this human experience; however, your argument makes me comprehend that, when all is said and done, I am experiencing the fleeting relative. On the other hand, what can I do if I am inclined to interpret life in terms of thinking, feeling and sex?

R - We said that a relative phenomenon is a simple contingent that follows the laws of its own existence. *Māyā* is movement, whether it be thought, emotion, instinct or form; it is not a question of taking or leaving it, but of comprehending it. If we realize that the relative has barely time to exist before it no longer is, what can we expect from it? Our identification with *māyā* brings us, sooner or later, to experience conflict, tension, self-assertion, strife, war and many other aberrations.

Possession, whether physical, psychological or spiritual, stems from identification with the world of the relative— which *is* and is not—therefore, with the world of *māyā*. To resolve identification with what one is not means putting an end to the strife between man and man, means emerging at last from human conflict.[2]

---

[1] See also the chapter "What is intended by Reality," in Raphael, *Tat tvam asi, op. cit.*

[2] See also the chapter "Sensory Life is Conflict," in Raphael, *Tat tvam asi, op. cit.*

Q - Do you believe that the materialist is bound to consider the relative real because he must justify his materialistic and phenomenal concept of life?

R - The materialist, so as not to contradict his identification with relative phenomena, must arrive at the extreme and absurd conclusion of considering a simple mirage real. On the other hand, he has no way out; he is tied down by his own inability to "see beyond."

— Which means that if a person has two-dimensional sight, he interprets life in two-dimensional terms, and that if someone speaks to him of three-dimensionality, he refuses to comprehend or accept it because he cannot see it?

R - Yes, that is how things stand.

— If I desire and experience without identifying myself with the world of *māyā*, can I solve my existential problems and my relationship with my fellow man?

R - If you wish to experience, that means that there is in you an impulse, an urge for certain experiences. The first factor we are faced with is your impulse-desire seeking gratification; furthermore, you claim that you would like to experience and desire without identification. If I am not mistaken, the picture is the following: on the one hand, there is a desire seeking gratification, and on the other, dis-identification with the gratifying desire; but these two movements annul each other.

Q - And are we not told that one may produce action without attachment to action? The *Bhagavadgītā* teaches something in this regard.

R - That is right. There is a pure kind of action that can be performed, but one must remember that it is not born of egoistic desire-impulse. Arjuna, in the *Gītā*, performs an action that does not belong to the individual, utilitarian or particular sphere; he fulfills a *dharma* of the *universal* order.[1]

From this point of view, we have pure action, which is given rise by an appropriate and depersonalized *instrument*; besides, it does not produce individual or egoistic fruits.

Now, the fruit of desire is the enjoyment of possessing, and if we are the prisoners of the one, we are also the prisoners of the other. An action born of desire is always egoistic, egoic or individual, as one may prefer to call it.

Q - (a previous questioner) Does this mean that if I wish to live and have experience, I am selfish? Is my desire to live utilitarian?

R - Do not see this word in moralistic and disparaging terms. One might put the question this way: I am urged on by "gratifying desires"; therefore, I like to live.

— I would also like to give.

---

[1] See *Bhagavadgītā: The Celestial Song*, Translation from the Sanskrit and Commentary by Raphael (New York: Aurea Vidyā, 2012).

R - But what can you give if you yearn for gratification and therefore yearn to take?

Giving in the true sense is a part of that pure action we spoke about before.

You must decide whether to take or give, because the two actions stem from different assumptions and from different standpoints in consciousness.

— So, one cannot want without desiring?

R - Is it possible to buy a car without desiring one?

Is it possible to desire sex without sexual desire?

Is it possible to move without desire to move?

Desire implies movement or direction toward something, while non-desire means staying still. These two states neutralize one another.

Q - Excuse me for interrupting, but I would like to ask if the relative, or *māyā* as you call it, can give me completeness and fullness? I am looking for completeness and fullness of being, because it seems to me, after all is said and done, that this is what we are all really aiming at.

R - This is a pertinent question. Let us examine it thoroughly. We saw before that the one Reality has *various degrees* of truth.[1] We also saw that these degrees of truth are contingent, fleeting and even contradictory. However, they can be perceived.

---

[1] See the chapter "Real and Non-real," in Raphael, *The Pathway of Non-duality: Advaitavāda, op. cit.*

Now, our problem is whether these degrees of truth, though experienced, are capable of bestowing completeness and fullness. We hold this to be fundamental; we might say to the friend who has just asked the question that this is what we are all really aiming at. Besides, it is not difficult to agree that the aim of the individual is that of finding his integral dimension, his fullness and true, authentic peace-happiness.

Thus, if the individual seeks his own fullness or realization, we may ask ourselves: can these degrees of truth, of *māyā*, bestow realization upon him?

Let us imagine an exterior datum expressing a certain degree of truth and bringing with it happiness or enjoyment. In order to obtain this happiness-fullness *persistently,* the individual requires two things:

1. That the exterior datum be constant and permanent.

2. That the individual always feels drawn toward that datum.

If one or both factors fail, then we must re-examine our hypothesis.

— On the basis of what we have said, it seems to me that there is no datum capable of bestowing true fullness. If all perishes, then my sensory happiness will perish too.

R - Well, supposing that such a datum did exist, what would the outcome be?

— That a being would fulfill itself through this external datum.

R - Certainly. So we must conclude that beings do not contain *in themselves* the possibility of completion. In other words, beings are wanting, incomplete and fragmentary. But if it is the *nature* of the being to be wanting and faulty, how can a datum, of whatever degree and dimension, change the *nature* of the being? We must agree that this is not possible; besides, such beings would live in a continuous state of dependence or subordination. In fact, the exterior datum, which should have represented only a marginal element, would acquire essential importance and worth.

Do you not think that a being is capable of completing itself in itself, that it may have a unitary and whole nature?

— I do. Otherwise we would have to change the concept of being, of entity.

R - Good. Now the being, in order to find itself again, must return into itself and abandon all identification with exterior data; that is, it must eliminate all the *supports* that constitute the continuity of the empirical ego, which alone is wanting and incomplete.

On the other hand, if knowledge is not within us, nobody can bestow it upon us; if beatitude is not within us, no one can offer it to us; if existence is not within us already, nobody can grant us the nature of being. If not within the seed, the flower can never bloom, exist or be.

We may conclude that true happiness-completeness, true knowledge, true unity-synthesis and the true constant are to be found in being itself, and that the aim of each single being is to seek the constant, to comprehend and be what we really are.

If one seeks true peace, which does not depend on objects or on any fleetingness whatsoever, then one must follow the Philosophy of Being.

Q - If I may, I would like to quote a few sentences I read in this book by Lama Anagarika Govinda, which states things that are different from what is held by *Asparśavāda*.

"There may be many levels or degrees of reality, but there cannot be any meaning in a "reality in itself"... a reality that is totally unrelated to anything, in other words, an absolute reality.

"...Since the Absolute is not derived from experience, but is merely the opposite of the relative, it has no reality whatsoever, nor has it any conceivable meaning or effect upon our lives or actions. Life means infinite relationship; the Absolute means the very contrary, and therefore the complete denial of life.... There is no death for those who admit the law of transformation.... The very fact that we are non-absolute beings in a non-absolute world gives us the freedom to experience this world in all its infinite aspects and life in all its infinite transformations."[1]

What can you say to such explicit statements?

---

[1] Lama Anagarika Govinda, *Creative Meditation and Multi-Dimensional Consciousness* (Wheaton, Ill.: Theosophical Publishing House, 1984).

R - Heraclitus made these same statements; for him all flows, becomes, transforms. Materialism itself down through the ages has always held that the only reality is the one we can experience through the senses and that an absolute that cannot be experienced by the senses is inconceivable; therefore, there is nothing new in what you say.

— But it is a Lama who writes these things when explaining the *vajrayāna* doctrine.

R - In any case, I believe it is subjective materialism.

— Can you tell me something about what I read?

R - We can all agree that certain things have been surpassed. Please bear in mind that we are not in the habit of entering into polemics with anyone. Our position of consciousness is one of total comprehending, and comprehension solves all problems.

— I have no intention of entering into polemics either, I simply wish to comprehend some points that, to tell the truth, perplex me too. That is why I ask you.

R - Let us say simply this: the denial of the Absolute is "stated" by that kind of thinking, which is itself relational, phenomenal, contingent and relative.
Relationship and movement mean duality, and duality—as stated elsewhere—cannot be the ultimate reality, because then we would find ourselves in a web of gaps and contradictions.

Besides, *denying* something also means stating it, and to deny the non-existent is silly.

— In other words, what you are saying is that if all is relative, then our statement cannot but be relative too?

R - Of course. It appears logical to me.

All that is stated or denied by a relative, phenomenal being cannot but be contingent and devoid of universal value. To claim that all is movement-nature means falling into panpsychism without any hope of escape; it means falling into absolutist phenomenalism, into a pantheism and, if taken to the extreme limit, into dangerous solipsism.

Śaṅkara holds that it is not possible to explain modification or the moments that follow one another without recognizing the existence of a sole, continuous and permanent principle that knows all things and is aware of the various changes.

On the other hand, if we regard movement-nature as real, then we also must recognize that all dualism, including pleasure-pain, is constant and eternal, and consider the thesis of those who seek liberation from conflict-suffering utterly unfounded. If, again, we claim movement-nature is simply a projection, conceptual representation or illusion devoid of a permanent substratum, then we must admit that an illusion cannot sustain another illusion. Yet absolute nihilism is unthinkable in both metaphysical and empirical terms.

Affirmation or negation of any datum is founded upon a conscious and knowing subject, in the face of which they are simple objects, they are a "second."

Q - But can the Absolute deny life, which is relationships and movement?

R - The Absolute can neither state nor deny; the individuality in *saṁsāra* denies and states because it places itself in a dualistic position.

Q - If we admit relativity, are we not implicitly recognizing absoluteness?

R - Yes. In order to know whether a body is moving, the idea of non-movement must be present in the mind-consciousness; otherwise, it would be impossible to know movement.

THE PHILOSOPHY OF BEING

Questioner - In the past you spoke in terms of Philosophy of Being; can you explain briefly what it consists of?

Raphael - It is not easy to explain it in just a few words. Remember that we have already spoken of it elsewhere.[1] The Philosophy of Being is the *Philosophia perennis* that deals with the Principles, but it can find its application in the contingent world as well. It is a Teaching that includes Transcendence and immanence, the Supranatural and the natural, the Immutable and the mutable.

— (same questioner) Are the Principles related to universal Life? Is this, then, a question of cosmogony?

R - I do not know what you mean by cosmogony; in any case, if you are referring to the doctrine dealing with the origin and formation of the universe, the Philosophy of Being does not refer to this alone, but goes beyond nature and the natured.

---

[1] See Raphael, *Which Democracy? References for a Good Government* (forthcoming from Aurea Vidyā, New York).

— But I think I read that manifestation is divided into three phases or *pāda*. Are these three distinct aspects of the One?

R - All branches of the Philosophy of Being speak of three universal aspects, plus a Fourth belonging to the metaphysical order.[1]

— In *Vedānta* these are called *Virāṭ, Hiraṇyagarbha* and *Īśvara*, are they not?

R - Yes. But one should remember that this triple division does not belong exclusively to *Vedānta*. Besides, it is not absolute. Unfortunately, the mind divides and separates what cannot be divided. The solar spectrum is composed of a sole light with varying vibratory modes; therefore, red is an integral part of that sole light. *Hiraṇyagarbha* is always *Īśvara* vibrating at different frequencies.

— What does the Philosophy of Being teach regarding the individual?

R - It teaches to Be rather than not to be. It teaches the individual in its entirety and totality. It teaches how to find oneself within oneself; it points out the illusions created by the mind, and it indicates the pathway of Realization and not the way of self-assertion or alienation as do the many philosophies invented by human imagination.

---

[1] See the chapter "The Three States of Being," in Raphael, *The Pathway of Non-duality, op. cit.*

— In brief, it teaches one how to find happiness within oneself?

R - More than that: it teaches one how to find in one's own heart Beatitude (*ānanda*), which is one's own *pax profunda* and Fullness. These could be the most effective terms to indicate the primeval state of being.

— If the Philosophy of Being leads to Beatitude, why do the majority, who desperately pursue happiness, not follow it?

R - Because they pursue the happiness of the senses, while this kind of Beatitude does not concern sensory being.

— Therefore, do we find ourselves at a crossroads: one road leads to supreme Good and the other to sensory good?

R - In a certain sense, this is so. The drive—that is, the pursuit of Goodness meant as Fullness—is the same in all men, but the pathways diverge. This is why we have the Philosophy of Being and that of becoming. The former indicates the road to Fullness and Beatitude that blossoms from the human heart's innermost recesses, while the latter points to a pathway of possession, alienation, externalization, of consumerism and estrangement from one's true Self. This is why the society of becoming is so full of dullness and escapism.

— Do you mean that the philosophy of becoming offers the anxious and anguished individual only the mirage of the golden calf?

R - In brief, yes. This kind of philosophy tries to tear the being away from himself, offering him the illusion of *objects* (it makes no difference what they may be: sex, cars, money, politics, etc.).

— Therefore the philosophy of becoming operates upon the plane of competition at all levels. Is that right?

R - Certainly, because it considers only externalized quantity. This is the cause of the obsession to have, to take, to possess even one's own exclusive and personal God, to increase, to accumulate desires and wealth. From this stem conflict, division, the struggle between the various social orders, as well as war.

— In what way can the Philosophy of Being resolve these conflicts and even wars?

R - By the very nature of the Philosophy of Being itself. For example, it would be sufficient to follow two principles in order to have a different view of human—and not only human—society. The first consists of the fact that the being, the individual, man, call him as you wish, contains within himself the possibility of being complete; therefore, he must not sell himself to anyone. The second considers that everything outside the individual is phenomena, mere instruments, a play of forms that come and go, appear, grow and vanish. This leads to a re-dimensioning of *objects*, to seeing them as what they really are.

Q - But does the philosophy of becoming not rest on these principles?

R - No, quite the contrary, my brother. With irrational and desperate strength, it does its utmost to urge the individual to *acquire,* and therefore to make a slave of him.

Forgive this apparent absolutism of mine, but in the society of becoming, all are slaves: slaves of the family, of the professions, of politics, of religion itself, of so-called culture, of competition, of distinction and of war.

— (previous questioner) So, is the Philosophy of Being applicable to both the plane of Principles and that of becoming? Is it a Teaching meant for man as a species and therefore for society? Besides, is it a Philosophy of harmony? I think I read this, if I am not mistaken.

R - Instead of struggles, of opposition and distinction, the Philosophy of Being proposes the harmony of one's self with oneself, of one's self with one's own species, of one's self with nature, because—among other things—It recognizes all realms of life as *entities* expressing Being. It is not, therefore, an anthropocentric but a cosmocentric Philosophy; this contains deep implications, which I feel all of you will be able to grasp.

— Some may think that the Philosophy of Being is a religion seeking to bestow psychological comfort.

R - There is no point in entering into the meaning of certain words; however, we can say that the Philosophy of Being is, first and foremost, Philosophy of Being. It is neither what is normally meant as a religion, nor is it a psychological theory or a form of individual conceptual philosophy in the Western sense.

Furthermore, it must be pointed out that it is the very philosophy of becoming that, by means of the illusion of *objects*, offers comfort and escape to the aimless "I" devoid of hope.

Q - The fact that you present *Vedānta* and *Asparśavāda* might lead one to believe that you wish to bring to the West a religion different from occidental ones.

R - I wish you to note that your question contains a number of errors of judgment.

First of all: We have not only spoken and written about *Vedānta* and *Asparśa*, but also about *Qabbālāh*, *Orphism* and *Platonism,* which are Western teachings.[1] During our conversations we have expounded the Doctrines of ancient Egypt, of Alchemy in the higher sense and of Buddhism. We have also explained that *Asparśa* is not in opposition to anything, on account of its transcendent character.

Secondly: *Vedānta* is not a religion in the Western sense; therefore, it is not correct to speak of a *Vedānta* religion.

Thirdly: *Asparśa* is metaphysics, and metaphysics be-longs neither to an individual nor to a people. Should we perhaps banish the music of Beethoven from Italy because

---

[1] For these Teachings, refer to the following works by Raphael: *The Pathway of Fire according to the Qabbālāh ('Ehjeh 'Ašer 'Ehjeh)*, *Orphism and the Initiatory Tradition* and *Initiation into the Philosophy of Plato* (New York: Aurea Vidyā; 1999, 2000 and 2005, respectively). For Alchemy, see the chapter "Fire of Life: Realization according to Alchemy," in Raphael, *The Threefold Pathway of Fire: Thoughts that Vibrate* (New York: Aurea Vidyā, 2000).

he was not an Italian? This is an absurd hypothesis. Music, like metaphysics, is universal, although it operates within a particular existential realm.

Fourthly: We have said that the Philosophy of Being is one only; therefore, the *Asparśavāda* teaching is simply one of Its particular *branches*.

Fifthly: The distinction between Christians, Muslims, Jews, Hindus, etc., is made by individuals from the society of becoming and not from that of Being; the same is true of the distinctions between East and West.

Q - I think that only in the West do the questions of political and religious exclusivity, intolerance and even racism arise.

R - Do not make an absolute of this concept. In any case, generally speaking, the Westerner, the European in particular, is strongly attached to his own traditions, and novelty frightens him. In India there is a great deal of religious tolerance and comprehension; many *credos* live alongside each other without opposition. Each one plays its own part, because, after all, there is room for all.

Q - If the philosophy of becoming embraces only non-being, does the Philosophy of Being embrace both Being and non-being?

R - Yes, this idea is correct. The Philosophy of Being is one of totality, synthesis and inclusion of the Whole. That is why it does not create opposition, distinction and conflict, and not only at the human level.

The philosophy of becoming is a philosophy of exclusion, one-sidedness, totalitarianism and alienation; it interprets the individual only in terms of desire and needs, of belly and sperm. For the philosophy of becoming, the individual is a compound of cells producing energy-work, a *robot* belonging to the context of machines; all he requires is two pounds of bread and other foodstuffs a day and the odd plaything to keep him happy. A body, whether human or animal, simply requires a certain number of calories per day. What else could it possibly need? This is why a number of ideologies of becoming believe that individuals can be disciplined, organized, marshalled and led by a handful of electronic brains, whether human or purely mechanical.

Q - Do you believe that some day humanity will become aware of its limitations and bonds? That it will free itself?

R - Look, it is very difficult to free an individual, however paradoxical this may seem.

As we said before, individuals prefer the happiness of the senses to that of the Being within them. Then there is another determining factor: the Princes of every tendency do all they can to prevent awareness of freedom. Slaves who love slavery need masters, and these in turn need slaves.[1] This is a kind of dualism, which unfortunately completes itself marvelously; at certain levels it represents a vital necessity, and whoever does not play along is ban-

---

[1] See the chapter "Idol Projection," in Raphael, *Which Democracy?*, *op. cit.*

ished from this society, often imprisoned or shut up in a mental asylum. Anyway, there is no cause for despair: in every epoch there have been individuals who, openly or secretly, have taken flight and tasted that peace that knows no conflict, that freedom that knows no desire.

Q - Speaking of the Philosophy of Being, sometimes you have said that the individual thrives on projections or superimpositions. Now I ask, of what exactly do these projections consist?

R - When, for example, we observe a sunset, we should stand still in pure contemplation without seeking to superimpose upon that reality concepts that, on the contrary, are the fruit of the mind's fancy. It is one thing to *contemplate* a sunset, another to imagine the event. Rather than contemplate, we usually imagine; the mind, with its recollections and classifications, disturbs contemplation.

— Does this mean eliminating personal considerations?

R - Yes. Wherever there is pure attention or awareness, there is contemplation and comprehension.

— Is this the reason why, generally speaking, the Scriptures fail to follow any kind of mental logic?

R - The empirical mind is greedy for philosophical, scientific, theological and political "systems" and so on; it is greedy for logical, deductive, inductive and consequential frames, and when it fails to find them, it becomes frustrated. Some of the cultures of the past are regarded by the empirical, systematic mind as being pre-logical. Fortunately, the individual of the past did not live by schemes, systems and by logical inductions, but by contemplation, direct experience and by union with life. Today we have very little contact with truth, but conversely we have many theoretical schemes and logical systems, which satisfy only the mind.

It could be that a logical, rational, consequential mind refuses our meetings because it fails to find an A, B, C, D, E, etc., scheme, but a B, D, A, C one instead. This mortifies the mind and irritates it because when deprived of its so-called logic, it remains without supports. But this is the very aim of this particular dialogue: the mind needs to be set aside. Life is not past, then present, then future; nor is it one, two, three, four, etc. Life is Present, it is Unity.

— Therefore the Philosophy of Being is not a logical and systematic philosophy?

R - No. Nor could it be, because Being is pure consciousness without superimpositions, because Being is not an entity that creates theoretical systems, constructions and schemes. Even the word Doctrine itself is misleading. In any case, the Philosophy of Being is not alogical or irrational, nor pre-logical, but supralogical.

Q - It seems to me, however, that the Philosophy of Being expresses itself in terms of past, present and future. What, for example, are the various *yugas* or the cosmic cycles?

R - We said elsewhere that the four *yugas* (epochs) represent states of consciousness.[1] This implies that today, while some experience the state of *kaliyuga*, others experience that of *satyayuga*. The four ages are all in the eternal present; the centuries co-exist, and it is the mind that divides them up, making a simple fraction of the absolute.

— One more question, if I may. Are the three states of waking, dream and deep sleep, spoken of in the *Māṇḍūkya Upaniṣad*, separate states?

R - No, they are not. The three states are three different modes illuminated by the *ātman*-Constant. The first two are characterized by cause-effect and by subject-object; the third, because the effect is potential, by cause alone, that is, by the subject resting within itself (from which may spring the peace of *samādhi*). In the first two states, there is mediated and relational knowledge and therefore contradiction; in the third, there is synthetic and immediate self-knowledge. But in *Turīya*, the Fourth, which illuminates the entire spectrum of the three states, there is neither cause nor effect, neither subject nor object, neither mediated nor immediate knowledge.[2]

---

[1] See the chapter "Social Orders," in Raphael, *Which Democracy?*, op. cit.

[2] For an in-depth review of these states of Being, see Gauḍapāda, *Māṇḍūkyakārikā: The Metaphysical Path of Vedānta*, Translation from the Sanskrit and Commentary by Raphael (New York: Aurea Vidyā, 2002), especially *sūtra* VII of the *Āgama Prakaraṇa*.

KARMA, SĀDHANĀ AND CULTURALISM

Questioner - I think I have *karma* that is not exactly favorable to Realization. Must I resign myself to this and put my Liberation off?

Raphael - *Karma* belongs to the egoistic phantom that "appears" and "disappears"; therefore, there is no reason to put off Realization of Self, because you are already this Self. What difficulties and who can prevent you from becoming aware of the fact that you are already the Self?

— (same questioner) It is this *karma* that creates the impediment.

R - *Karma* is a product of the mind. If you make the mind vanish, *karma* too will vanish.
Whoever *is* already has no cause for procrastination.

Q - Inevitably the world that surrounds us represents a great obstacle to our *sādhanā*; sometimes it prevents us from fulfilling our *dharma* as disciples.
What can be done to solve this state of affairs?

R - All obstacles we meet are neither absolute nor determined. An obstacle is such if the mind considers it so.

Q - We are going through the darkest period of the *kaliyuga*, and this forces us more than ever to retreat and be absorbed by the overpowering materialism.

How can we emerge from this imprisoning situation?

R - There are neither *kaliyuga*s nor *satyayuga*s when it comes to the Self. All names and forms are simply a product of the descriptive mind. It is sufficient to silence the mind to cause the world of names and forms to disappear. *Kaliyuga* and *satyayuga* are states of consciousness.

Q - Can you propose a *tapas* and a *sādhanā* capable of freeing me from the negative family situation I am experiencing at the moment?

R - *Sādhanā* and *tapas* are norms, austerities, psycho-physical attitudes that aim at obtaining a future effect. Now, in order to reach awareness of Self, it is sufficient to *recall* that one is Self. We are here in Rome, and if one of you were to ask me the road to Rome, I would simply answer that there is no need for a road because you are here already. One must simply become aware of the state of things. One must *recognize* a reality that has always existed and that requires nothing to be achieved and revealed.

Q - I have very few years left to live, and I believe that an intense *sādhanā* may be of use to me. What do you advise?

R - Reality, the Constant, the Self cannot have just a few years of life left; otherwise, what do we mean when we say that a datum is Real?

A Constant must remain constant; otherwise, it is no longer a constant. Do you not agree?

— So what can I do?

R - You must remove from your consciousness the false idea that you will die, that you will perish, that you have only a few years left.

— This prospect consoles me, but even if my mind considers me a constant, I find that my health and strength are failing me.

R - The mind, being time-space, cannot but interpret life in terms of time and space. The awareness we are speaking about is not of the manasic order. Whose is the poor health, to whom does it belong? Who suffers, who dies and is born?

— Are you asking me?

R - Certainly. This is a dialogue.

— My poor health belongs to my physique, to my body.

R - In your statement there are two terms to ponder: *my* and *body*. We have, therefore, a body that belongs to an *ego*. The ill health belongs to the body and not to the self. If you are the Self, what does the body, as a simple superimposition, have to do with it?

Q - But it is often said that the ego itself is an illusion!

R - That is true. But now we are simply examining your ego in relation to your body, not to your Self.

— Is it sufficient to consider oneself immortal in order to become immortal?

R - It is not a question of "considering oneself" and "becoming." You are an existent, and therefore there is no reason for "considering oneself" such or for endeavoring to "become" existent. Who *is* must simply *comprehend* that, in fact, he *is*. Nothing else is necessary.

— Science tells us that we have evolved from the animal state and that in our present state we cannot consider ourselves absolute, that it will take us several million years to become complete.
How can I possibly be in an instant what I will be in a million years' time?

R - Reality as such does not depend either upon time, space or cause-effect. This topic was already discussed in the *Māṇḍūkya Upaniṣad* and other sources.

— I do not understand this properly. Could you explain more precisely what you mean?

R - Reality, or the Self, does not evolve. The Absolute, if dependent on time-space, is not Absolute but is a simple contingency. The Absolute has neither birth, nor evolution, nor death.

— But has the individual, since his first appearance upon this planet, not evolved? This fact appears evident to me.

R - He has simply developed some of his individual phenomenal faculties. But individuality, however much it expands or improves, can never unveil the Self, *ātman* or Being, because these are beyond all development and motion.

Being belongs to a different order from that of the empirical ego, however much it may expand its explicative modalities. From a metaphysical point of view, one might say that the individual has gone through an *involution*, not an *evolution*.

— Therefore, you consider the scientific theories of evolution false?

R - I do not say that they are correct or incorrect. I simply hold that Being as such does not evolve, because it *is* what it is, has been and always will be.

To say that Being is born or that it dies (evolutionism) means placing a contradiction within Being. Man, over time, has developed a number of psychic *faculties* and has grasped a number of the laws of the world of *māyā*.

Q - Is it easier for the intellectual, the person with an academic or other kind of culture, to comprehend this pathway? Is the ascesis-*sādhanā* of such a person swifter?

R - One's descriptive knowledge of the world of names
and forms is of little importance. What counts is having
the proper qualifications and a suitable intelligence.

An individual is no closer to God or to Truth because
he is an intellectual; on the contrary, it may happen that
he is actually farther away from them than those we define
as the ignorant. The approach to Truth does not stem from
the quantity of notions one has stored up in the mind.

Culture may be of help if it sets the intelligence in
motion. The individual who lacks culture may have a
tamasic mind. The great theologian or *paṇḍit* may be
anything but a saint, and, vice versa, the saint may not
be either a theologian or a *paṇḍit*. There are some who
have memorized the *Vedas* or the Christian Gospels and
simply talk about them, and some who live by the *Vedas*
and the Gospel without even knowing of their existence.
There are those who practice and experience Śaṅkara's
Vivekacūḍāmaṇi[1] without knowing Sanskrit, and those who
have a profound knowledge of Sanskrit and even translate the
Vivekacūḍāmaṇi without either living by it or realizing it.

Realization must defend itself from the magical occultism of *manas*, as well as from sterile intellectual verbiage.
What one must do is avail oneself of metaphysical intuition without falling into the metaphysics of concepts and
sophisms, which, however gratifying, does not lead to the
supraconceptual Supreme. When Tradition is brought down
to the sensorial, emotional and sentimental level and onto

---

[1] Śaṅkara, *Vivekacūḍāmaṇi: The Crest Jewel of Discernment*,
Translation from the Sanskrit and Commentary by Raphael (New York:
Aurea Vidyā, 2006).

the plane of intellectual conceptualism, it becomes simple literature and no longer the life of transfiguration.

In any case, culture has its validity when considered in its correct function. Culture, in its right meaning, should be aimed at *educating* our mind and consciousness. Unfortunately, many simply play with words, thoughts and concepts. Besides, we draw a distinction between culture and erudition.

Q - Science and technology have led man to live longer and given him access to a greater quantity of food.

These rather evident circumstances would alone suffice to show that science, or a kind of society based on science, is of extreme and irreplaceable importance.

R - I shall never cease to underline the fact that we are not against science, but against the exclusivist dictatorship of *scientism*. Science is *one* branch of the humanly knowable, and, as science, it has its place within the scheme of things. But the individual is not only a scientist; he is also a philosopher. He is a poet, an artist, etc.; he is also a spiritual and religious being. Being flies upon the wings of knowledge, love, faith, the will and the spirit. Its action is horizontal but also vertical. We cannot expect to turn all men, by force or suggestion, into philosophers, scientists, mystics or farmers.

On the other hand, the two points mentioned by you concern a kind of action addressed only to the individual's gross-physical body. But the human being is not merely a body although he obviously should know how to take care of it.

POINTS OF VIEW AND ERUDITION

Questioner - I notice that many adepts within the spiritual field claim the truth. And so we have the various kinds of *yoga*, the different *darśanas*, the various occultist, initiatory doctrines, and so on, of the West, all in disagreement and, I might add, all fighting each other. Thus, *Yoga* states that it alone is truthful, and so does *Sāṃkhya*, *Nyāya*, Sufism, the Rosicrucians, etc. Many followers and non-followers of the tradition, initiates and fervent activists of various spiritual currents, hold that they alone have truly grasped the truth while the others may have, if barely.[1] It is highly likely that some will claim that you are wrong or that you have understood very little. What have you to say in response to these people? My question may appear strange, but I do not think so; I would like to comprehend a mode of being that to date escapes me.

Raphael - To whom should I address my answer? I do not have a manasic mind that creates separation and duality. Where duality exists, distinction and opposition exist; but wherever there is Unity-without-a-second, there can be neither opposition nor separation.

---

[1] See the chapter "Shadows on the Gurus and the Cultural Traditionalists," in Raphael, *Which Democracy?, op. cit.*

In Gauḍapāda's *kārikās* 17 and 18, Chapter III of the *Māṇḍūkya Upaniṣad*, we read: "The dualists are firmly convinced of the different theses inherent in their own conclusions, [but they are forced] to contradict themselves reciprocally. [Instead] this [non-duality] is not in contradiction with anyone." "Because non-duality is the supreme truth, it can be maintained that duality is [an accidental possibility] of non-duality. For the dualists, there is a duality in both cases [absolute and relative]. For this reason, [non-duality] is not opposed [to the dualists]."

Again, in *kārikā* 5, Chapter IV, Gauḍapāda states: "...We comprehend [instead] this [vision] free from any dispute"[1]; and Śaṅkara in his commentary to the *kārikā* continues, "...For this reason, O disciples, comprehend the philosophy of the ultimate Truth, which is beyond all dispute."

— (same questioner) Does this mean that the *Asparśavāda* does not oppose the other *darśanas*?

R - The *Asparśavāda* is not in opposition because it recognizes that, in time-space, all possible points of view may be valid.

The *darśanas*—for *Asparśa* or *Advaita*—are degrees of truth that are annulled in the One-without-a-second. The *Advaita* "point of view" is of the universal order, and the universal cannot oppose anyone. All the contradictions emerge thanks to *māyā*, but they vanish when *māyā* is transcended.

---

[1] Gauḍapāda, *Māṇḍūkyakārikā, op. cit.*

In the point without dimension, as all distinction belonging to exterior points of view has been transcended and resolved, opposition disappears and Imperturbability alone reigns. When one realizes oneself as that point, *māyā* movement ceases to exist, so one no longer enters into conflict with anyone or anything whatsoever.

— Does this mean, therefore, that some create opposition or dualism because they have not achieved this *Advaita* or *Asparśa* dimension?

R - Seeing that you insist on the matter, we may even say this: there is *ascent* in order to realize *Brahman*, then there is *descent* to embrace the all.

— Could you explain that better?

R - During ascesis or ascent the individual, generally speaking, places himself in opposition to the "not this," that is, to the world of differentiation, and also to the various doctrines or individuals who think in a different way. When he realizes *Brahman*—that is, the Unity-without-a-second—he discovers that there is *nobody* to oppose, there is neither the just nor the non-just. Then, if he is a *jīvanmukta* (who is liberated in life), he re-descends, taking this reality with him, living by it, incarnating it. But this time he no longer opposes life, because he has assimilated into himself the "not this" that once represented his opposite and the "other." We can say that a truly freed person closes the book of the opposites of

life and places himself within *pax profunda* or Beatitude
without objects.[1]

Q - Ramana Maharsi—whom I have known—always
placed himself in a dual position, because he understood
that those he spoke to were unable at that particular
moment to grasp *Advaita* truth. That is, he did not oppose
the dualistic point of view of his questioner. Only now do
I comprehend why he did not contradict. I now realize
that the position of the truly liberated person is different
from that of the individual veiled by *māyā* and also from
the simple spiritualistic intellectual.

The Liberated one has no need to demonstrate anything dialectically or to defend a theory, however worthy
and sublime. Is what I say correct?

R - For the Liberated one, the book of the polarity of
life has been closed; therefore he is Silence. Comprehension of the true and the false, of the just and the unjust,
of good and evil, of Tradition and non-Tradition and of
the superior and the inferior implies that there is nothing
left to say or do.

The Liberated one need not defend anything or anyone;
the Liberated one reveals himself, and that is all. He may
not even speak of *Asparśa*, of *Advaita*, of *darśana* or of
Tradition. A Liberated one is beyond all theoretical argu-

---

[1] For the condition of a *jīvanmukta* or "liberated in this life," see
ślokas 427-444, in Śaṅkara, *Vivekacūḍāmaṇi, op. cit.*, and the chapter
"Jīvanmukta," in Raphael, *At the Source of Life: Questions and Answers
concerning the Ultimate Reality* (New York: Aurea Vidyā, 2001).

ment, all cultural debate, all demonstration and all doctrine. Ramana was one of these. He was a living "book."

The Liberated one is law unto himself because *Brahman* has no law other than that which springs from its
own nature.

Q - Therefore, wherever there is "I'm right, you're
wrong," "I'm black and you're white," is there discursive-
ness and simple "opinion"?

R - All these things belong to and are perpetuated in
the world of *māyā*.

There are people who ascend by means of emotion-
sentiment, and others by means of intellect and will; but
as long as they are ascending, they remain within the dual
and within opposition. Once *Brahman*, the One-without-a-
second, is realized, their consciousness embraces the All;
thus they lay down all thought, emotion and action and
live only in fullness and completeness.

Q - I follow *Advaita* because there are many valid
reasons for considering it as the way of the supreme Reality, the only way leading to Peace and all-comprehending
Silence. My difficulty in following *Advaita* is found in
the intellectual energy that forces me to create opposition upon the dialectical plane, to make distinctions and
at times to engage in crusades. I am often attracted, by
way of tuning, to certain writers who place themselves in
a critical position; I too have written something along the
same lines. But in moments of illumination, I recognize
that the true path, if one seeks realization, is that of total
transcendence of the intellect, because all theories and all

teachings are simply multiple aspects of the whole Truth. The intellect, like sentiment, is duality.

Therefore, I have come to the conclusion, something I did not accept in the past, that only the company of the Realized and the Liberated is capable of urging the consciousness of the aspirant to achieve the Silence that allows no duality. Do you agree with me? Have you anything to add?

R - I agree, and I do not really have anything to add. Let us read these verses by Gauḍapāda:

"The *ātman* is imagined as *prāṇa* and other indefinite things. This is due to the *māyā* of the resplendent (*ātman*) through which it reveals itself."

"...Those who know the *bhūtas* call *ātman*-reality *bhūtas*; those who know the *guṇas* call reality *guṇas*; those who know *tattvas* call reality *tattvas*."

"...The knowers of the *lokas* consider *ātman*-reality the *lokas*, and the adorers of *Devas* consider only the *Devas* to be real."

"Those who know the *Vedas* call *ātman*-reality the *Vedas*, while those who make sacrifices call reality the sacrifices..."

"Those who know the subtle sphere define *ātman*-reality as subtle; those who know the gross sphere call the gross plane reality. Those who adore a Person, under any form whatsoever, consider that Person reality, and those who do not believe in any form call reality the emptiness."

"Those who know time call *ātman*-reality time... Those who know debate call reality the debate..."

"Some maintain that *ātman*-reality is composed of twenty-five categories, some of twenty-six, some of thirty-one, while others believe the categories to be countless."

"...and others know It as *para* (supreme) and as *apara* (non-supreme)."

"Those who know creation consider *ātman*-reality creation those who know dissolution (*laya*) describe reality as dissolution, and those who believe in conservation call it conservation. All these ideas are simply images projected (by the *jīvātman*)."[1]

As a piece of rope in the half-light may be mistaken for a snake, a garland, a stick, etc., so too the incommensurable *Brahman-ātman*, on account of *māyā*, is mistaken for *Īśvara*, for *Virāṭ*, for the *Devas*, for the *Vedas* and for all the form-images that the projecting *manas* is capable of ideating.

— Do you think that assessment, judgment and classification always involve belittlement of others and glorification of oneself?

R - Depending upon the motive, at certain levels "verdicts" and condemnations, for any reason whatsoever, are to be banished.[2]

---

[1] *Kārikās* 19-28, Chapter II, Gauḍapāda, *Māṇḍūkyakārikā*, *op. cit.*

[2] See the chapter "Scourgers and Executioners," in Raphael, *Which Democracy?*, *op. cit.*

A heart that expands to the point of brushing the circumference ceases to oppose, judge, pronounce sentences and condemn.

Q - I wish to go back to a question asked a little while back. For twenty years I went through the various levels of the education system, and I have been teaching for fifteen years. And yet I am more and more convinced that, as there is no limit to erudition, one remains ignorant.

If this ignorance is our *karma*, how can we emerge from it?

R - You speak of erudition, and this we accept; we find the term appropriate. Erudition is a mass, a heap of cognitions that refer to the world of names and forms, that is, to becoming.

Now, becoming, precisely because it is becoming, cannot but be full of fluctuating relative and contingent notions that change, transform themselves and can also be annulled by other notions. In becoming, knowledge is not absolute but relative, and the relativity of erudition makes the individual relative too.

Truth is not to be found in the relative or in change; therefore an encyclopedic erudition, however great, does not put an end to ignorance and thus to conflict.

Knowledge, with a capital K, is not based upon becoming and its fleeting process, but upon the Principles underlying the becoming-process, those principles that are universal and imperishable. Thus Knowledge is stable, and in it the individual himself finds stability and strength. As this principial Knowledge is synthetic knowledge, it concerns the oneness of life, and oneness and synthesis are neither quantity nor dispersion. Knowledge cannot be measured in terms of verbal quantity; therefore, it does not belong to the discursive, dianoetic order.

You may feel ignorant because you have partaken of this kind of erudition, which yields no synthesis, permanence or stability. It is up to you, comprehending, to forsake the erudition of becoming and to enter the Knowledge of Being.

— Yes, I understand. I have even noticed that erudition inflates the ego and feeds many of its attributes.

R - We are convinced of this. Erudition creates pride, separateness, power, capital and a sense of superiority, and also conflict and sorrow.

— Must I therefore fight erudition?

R - It is not a question of fighting; it is a question of putting things in their proper place. For the ego, this is very difficult.

— Pardon my question: do you feel erudite?

R - Raphael, rather than *doing*, favors *contemplation*. But this is neither inertia, nor listlessness, nor passivity; unfortunately, in the West certain terms have become degenerate or are misunderstood. Writing itself, for example, is already *doing*.

Raphael often says that to write about *Brahman* is not the same as being realized. Some think they are Masters because they are prolific like rabbits and full of mental concepts. One needs to be humble, but also courageous. One must abandon the "power" of erudition and the fruits that derive from it. Where there is erudition, there is ego; there is a samsaric phantom and memory. There is also arrogance, presumption and a sense of superiority. The erudite are imprisoned in their own cultural theories. I think you must have experienced all this.

— A final question. Perhaps it is rather strange, but for me it is not. In any case you are free not to answer. Have you ever been gratified by an offensive epithet?

R - When one emerges from the "cave," one is usually thrown to the wild beasts, especially here in the West.

— But the wild beasts eat carrion.

R - Exactly. But whosoever is *ātman*, eternally non-born, non-caused and non-formed, does not fear their teeth, nor does he feel them.

ORIGINAL SIN AND CHRISTIANITY

Questioner - From the point of view of the Self, has the so-called "fall" its own reality, or should one not even take the problem into consideration?

Raphael - From the point of view of the Self, there is neither going nor coming, neither fall nor ascent.

— (same questioner) So how can we define this state of *avidyā*? How can we define the state we experience?

R - This state means identification with the line or mode of expressive life. We may speak of fallen beings only when we become aware and consider that experience absurd. We can say that we have made a mistake when we recognize our error.

— Therefore, is human experience (the "fall") simply an experience among many? A way of life?

R - It is one of the multiple modes of life, neither better nor worse than the others; therefore, it should not be rejected.

— Is it only when a person comprehends or, better still, when he tires of experience, that he begins considering things differently?

R - As long as we remain identified, we have no possibility of vision. For the person who identifies himself with the "snake" projection, the snake will always remain snake. It is when the projection slows down and with it identification that one may notice the rope in the snake's place.

Q - Can we state that the "fall" means finding oneself limited by and enclosed within a circumference?

R - If one day a person *imagines* himself to be a plant, we might say he "fell" into *avidyā*.

— What would be the best way to live in this world of *māyā*?

R - To be in *māyā*, to use *māyā*, but not be of *māyā*. In other words, to be in the world, but not of the world.

Q - If the "fall" means having entered into the individualized dimension, then is human experience against nature?

R - Human experience is, as we said before, one of the many experiences of Life. In and of itself, it is neither better nor worse than any other. Being, however, is not human individuality alone; it is something more. We may say that the "fall" represents a split of being.[1]

When the reflection of incarnated consciousness identifies with formal multiplicity, it causes dispersion; however, the fact remains that it may be a precise experience of life.

Q - I am a Christian, and according to this tradition the "fall" represents in actual fact separation from God.

Saint Thomas writes: "Thanks to original justice, reason perfectly controlled the lower powers of the soul and was in turn perfected by God to whom it was subject. This original justice was lost because of the first man's sin. So, all the soul's powers were thus deprived of the order that naturally inclined them to virtue."

Is this in keeping with what has been said here?

R - The essence is the same; the words change, but words are of little importance.

Original sin did not totally sunder the umbilical cord that unites the creature and the Creator; it merely weakened and confounded it so that the creature forgot the Parent.

Q - Could you, if you do not mind, explain this truth in philosophical terms?

---

[1] See the chapter "The Fall of the Soul," in Raphael, *The Pathway of Non-duality: Advaitavāda, op. cit.*

R - We have already treated this question briefly.[1]
Vedānta might say that between Being and being there is
māyā; integrate this, and you achieve reintegration.

Q - (the second-last questioner) This is the same as
saying that between the Creator and the creature there
is original sin; integrate this, and reintegration has been
achieved. Is my conclusion correct?

R - It is the same thing, even though theological in-
terpretations may vary.

— Can original sin be dissolved and cancelled by the
submission of man to God?

R - It is not a question of passive, sentimental submission. It is said that Christ came into the world to
strengthen the weakened link, to re-establish the parent-
child covenant. Between the Creator and the creature
who seeks reintegration, there is Christ, the intermediary
capable of mending the split.

— Therefore, Christ alone may solve the problem of
this split or "fall"?

R - It is important to comprehend what Christ
represents. Christ is a name that conceals a *principle-quality*, whereby, in final analysis, this principle-quality unites and shortens the distance. We can

---

[1] For other references, see the chapter "Solution of the Energy
Complex," in Raphael, *Which Democracy?, op. cit.*

say that Jesus incarnated this principle and revealed this quality. What did the historical Jesus incarnate?

— I continue to think of man's submission to God.

— (another questioner) The second person of the Trinity?

— (yet another questioner) I think He incarnated love. Did Christ not come to bring this new Commandment, which had been excluded from the Old Testament?

R - Good. He incarnated Love; therefore, Love is that principle-quality that strengthens what has been weakened, that principle that shortens the distance between Being and non-being until it disappears altogether.

Between the Principial and the individualized, or human egotism, lies Love; with Love, egotism-selfishness is transfigured into inclusiveness. Through Love, the individual is dissolved into the universal and then into the Principle.

— But is it not Jesus who washes "sin" away? "Lamb of God who washes away the sins of the world..."?

R - I do not wish to think that we are falling into a condition of alienation. Many Christians have projected the instrument of salvation outside of themselves. If we recognize the fact that the Kingdom of Heaven is within us and that Christ-Love must take root and grow within the depths of our own nature, then we shall be in harmony with the teachings of *Premayoga*, the *yoga* of Love.[1]

— But Jesus is the son of God; indeed, he is God himself who has come into the world.

R - In fact, Love is the substance of God, and this Love existed before the worlds were, because it was in God. Intelligence also is substance of God. God is *sat-cit-ānanda*.

— If I am not mistaken, you mean to say that what is in relation to the entity Jesus should be in relation to Love? In other words, must one look not at the individual, but at the Quality incarnated by the individual?

R - The ordinary individual does not see beyond forms. Therefore he interprets reality in terms of individuality. If we continue along these lines, it is possible to arrive at an individualistic and materialistic kind of religion. But God is Spirit and must be adored as such, so the Scriptures say.

Furthermore, one must keep the following in mind: it is infantile, easy and nothing exceptional to adore a form and believe that it can do everything for us. But to follow the text "Be perfect as your Father in Heaven is perfect" is very difficult. Perfect Love reveals itself only when we *die* to ourselves, when individuality is nailed to the Cross

---

[1] See *Initiation into the Mysteries of Love* in the chapter "Bhakti-yoga," in Raphael, *Essence and Purpose of Yoga: The Initiatory Pathways to the Transcendent* (Shaftesbury, Dorset: Element Books, 1996).

of redemption, when we admit—no longer as children, but as adults—that if we do not ascend the mount of transfiguration, our ego with all its products will be unable to dissolve or die. Therefore we must pay great attention not to fall into quietism.

Q - How can it be that in two thousand years Love has failed to operate, seeing that today the majority of people are materialistic and selfish?

R - Love has rarely been expressed, and the little that has been has appeared in sentimental, therefore paternalistic, terms.

The Love we are talking about is not sentiment; it is a universal principle, and it can be achieved insofar as the individual and the particular are transcended. "Only the pure of heart shall see God."

Q - Do you think the Christian religion is superior, inferior or equal to other religions?

R - Live Love, express Love, incarnate Love, and then tell me if life can be interpreted in terms of superiority or inferiority, mine and yours, pride and separation.

Q - I believe that Christianity is the way of Love, Judaism is the way of the Law, Hinduism is the way of Wisdom and Buddhism is the way of *Dharma*, but they all express aspects of the one Reality.

R - Yes, I think so too.

TRANSFORMATION OF CONSCIOUSNESS
AND TECHNIQUES

Questioner - You often say that we should transform our consciousness, but transformation implies change, and change—and you always say this—is conflict. Besides, transformation means following a model, and to follow a model, I think, implies imprisonment because it means entering into duality. So how can we transform ourselves?

Raphael - It is important that we "comprehend each other." Although certain things cannot be conceptualized or described, nonetheless we need to communicate, and, alas, the instruments at our disposal only permit us to communicate verbally. Let us use an example.

Today we have a kind of "awareness" that sees a "snake" where there is a "rope"; this awareness of vision is so rooted in us that *consciousness* and *view* become one and the same, to the point of making admission of the contrary, or the acceptance of another view, impossible. Because this is a rooted aspect of our consciousness—therefore not simply a notion perceived by our peripheral senses— this consciousness-view must be transformed, and the world we see, feel and experience must be utterly revolutionized.

It is not, therefore, a question of transforming oneself into another "projection," thus perpetuating the former state of ignorance, but of recovering awareness of what one really is.

Realization means being fully conscious of Reality. Individual empirical consciousness is only a part or, better, a reflection of universal Consciousness (*cit*). Thus, it is necessary to transform one's erroneous view and, naturally, to liberate that part of one's consciousness that adheres to it. Or, if you like—because it is simply a question of our understanding one another—to transform one's crystallized, institutionalized viewpoint.

If, for example, the crystallized "snake" view is replaced by a view of a "garland," a "stick," a "trickle of water," etc., we find ourselves in the condition you referred to: that is, we transform ourselves into something other than ourselves ("rope"). This kind of transformation is becoming, is process, is prison. Erudition operates in this manner. Instead, what counts is that the transformation (= going beyond form-projection) is such as to impede the birth of any projection-image whatsoever, because Being is beyond the world of names and forms. The *rope,* in our example, is not a stick, a garland, a serpent or a trickle of water, etc. If someone tells us that, even though he has recognized this reality, he still lives as a "snake" and not as a *rope,* we would reply that this occurs because the profound transformation of consciousness, capable of dissolving the snake-phantom, has not happened.

We have often said that the majority *are not* because they experience simple representations, simple notions.

— (same questioner) Therefore, if I have grasped the idea properly, consciousness should not shift into various other projections but should resume its proper state of Being. Thus, if Being is immortal, and the reflection of incarnate consciousness does not believe itself to be such, what it must do is recognize its own immortality and remember to be immortal. If I am not mistaken, this corresponds to Plato's "reminiscence."

Getting back to the "model" to follow, I was referring to *sādhanā*, to the various techniques, etc.

To what extent can techniques lead me to Being? Do the various techniques have an intrinsic value of their own, or are they used simply to stun?

R - *Asparśavāda* and *Advaita Vedānta* represent the direct pathway because they seek essentially to transform the consciousness, without any kind of mediation.

If we merely repeat the *mantra "Tat tvam asi"* (That thou art) in litany fashion, we simply provoke, as Śaṅkara states, a slight straining of the vocal cords. This *mantra* should be taken in the immediacy of integral comprehension; that is, the consciousness should grasp, comprehend and recognize the truth underlying it.[1] Meditation, therefore, consists in intuiting the essence of the *mantra*.

As far as the different techniques used by the various kinds of *yoga* and *sādhanā* are concerned, we can say that, as techniques, they are *means* (at times quite valid) that help the individual in his *sādhanā*. To say that a technique leads to *Brahman* is too much. However, to state that a technique is of no use is going too far in the

---

[1] For a deeper comprehension of the *mantra* "Tat tvam asi," refer to *ślokas* 241-253, in Śaṅkara, *Vivekacūḍāmaṇi, op. cit.,* and to Part II, Chapter XVIII ("That Thou Art: Tat tvam asi prakaraṇam"), in Śaṅkara, *Upadeśasāhasrī.*

opposite direction. Everything must be put into proper perspective. Unfortunately, the mind often resorts to extremes.

There are those who approach the Doctrine in an intellectual fashion, and, creating the excuse that techniques are of no use, seek realization through simple and sterile indoctrination. On the contrary, there are others who abhor dianoetic intellectualism and seek only techniques, whereby they lose themselves in technicalities as ends in themselves.

We shall say that *Brahman* does not depend either on techniques, of any type or degree whatsoever, or on manasic intellect because It cannot be determined or conditioned by simple empirical supports. But it is equally true that the individual who identifies with his projections is free to use all means capable of favoring awareness of his true Essence.

Q - There are instructors who refuse *in toto* all doctrines, philosophy, scripture, religion, techniques and all kinds of teaching. Do you think it is possible to achieve realization without any of these supports?

R - I think this is a form of extremism and that all forms of extremism and absolutism on the empirical plane lead to the opposite effect.

Besides, it is not the doctrines, philosophies or instructors that need to be eliminated; we must simply correct our own approach to them.

— Do you mean that it is not by refusing this or that, that we can find a proper approach to things?

R - Yes, certainly. We cannot refuse certain outlets to the soul that places itself upon the plane of pure research, of pure investigation, or pure knowledge.

— Why then do these people reject reading of any kind?

R - Perhaps it depends upon their preoccupation with the fact that many read simply for the sake of self-erudition, or that the individual tends to follow the line of least resistance, which is that of objectifying knowledge.

Q - Some claim that language itself is an impediment to realization. But how can we communicate through verbal silence?

R - We have said so too. But, we repeat, we should not make what cannot be an absolute into an absolute. At the empirical, individual level of the *manas*, we cannot communicate except through language.

We know that the word *Īśvara*, for example, expresses a precise state of being, a consciential reality. If we stop short at a simple verbal expression as such, we merely memorize a word, a concept, which, in truth, is of little use. But, if this word is conceived as a *symbol* of an authentic reality or "experience" of life, then everything changes. Thus, language and, above all, symbols are *instruments* of realization.

Q - Already the *Upaniṣads* say that intellectual culture is of no use, and they let it be comprehended that realization alone is capable of creating identity with *Brahman*;

therefore, why do some refuse the scriptures when these speak so clearly?

R - Once more, if there is a proper approach to the Doctrine, this cannot but be valid and act as a useful stimulus. Rather than refusing the Doctrine, which is knowledge of the Principle, one must teach, first of all, the proper approach to the Doctrine.

Q - There are some *gurus*, as we've already mentioned, who hold that they have neither doctrine, nor method, nor technique, nor any other kind of instrument through which to achieve realization because this would imprison and alienate. I've followed this principle for a while, but now I realize that I've simply been wasting my time. What do you advise me to do now?

R - We are still on the same problem. Very well! We will add more; at the individualized level, to seek to eliminate all operative instruments means to deprive oneself of the stimuli necessary for growth. On the empirical plane, to try to exclude language means not to communicate, and those who claim they refuse language not only defend a method—that of non-language—but are obliged to have recourse to language in order to teach it. All methods, doctrines, techniques, etc., lose their function when consciousness is reintegrated into *That*; but until one achieves *That*, to exclude the possibility of adequate stimulation means to lose oneself in inertia or apathy.

If there are different types of *yoga*, with different methods and techniques, this is because not everyone is in the same state of consciousness.[1] *Asparśavāda*, for example, is the "way without supports," that is, without psycho-physical props. However, it is a kind of *yoga* suited to those who have a non-formal, non-conceptual mind; in other words, those who have a *buddhi* filled with *sattva* are capable of comprehending it fully and realizing it.

To try to apply this *yoga* while one is polarized at the level of the objectifying *manas*, or of polar feeling, means creating psychological divisions. It must be presumed that the individual who approaches *Asparśa*—like, on the other hand, one who approaches *Zen*—has already *integrated* the feeling and perceiving of the *manas* into the *buddhi*, the supraconscious intuition.

Buddhi does not require conceptual reasoning—which, on the contrary, is stimulating for the *manas*—or a technique that rests on *manas* or feeling.

If, therefore, we favor a kind of *yoga* that transcends all forms of intraindividual psychic methodology, we should be able to comprehend those who sustain what you say. However, there is no need to make certain things absolute or to disregard that, in time and space, certain techniques may have validity for some people. We should recognize the fact that techniques as such do not imprison us; it is our mistaken approach to them that does. A technique can even break through certain circumferences and dissolve particular crystallizations.

A true Instructor tries to give each one what he needs, even if He himself is beyond *his own* technique, *his own* teaching, *his own* methods and *his own* thought. We must

---

[1] For an in-depth study of the various paths, see Raphael, *Essence and Purpose of Yoga, op. cit.*

remember that the Doctrine is not somebody's conceptual philosophy, that it does not belong to individuality.

Q - Allow me to ask this question: don't some, by trying to impose their own method, exploit a certain mode of expression?

R - Yes, I know what you mean. We have said elsewhere that there are many ways of making one's own idea, one's own doctrine, or methodology, etc., exclusive. There is also the fact that a number of *gurus* have adapted themselves to suit the present outlook, which seeks to desecrate everything and separate it from the Principle. However, I insist on the fact that in the universe there is nothing to accept or refute; what can enslave us is our erroneous approach to things.

Q - There is another fact that perplexes me, and it is this: some hold that certain teachings, including some traditional teachings, are outdated and obsolete. Now I wonder if the traditional Doctrine, if it is non-human, can ever become old-fashioned and obsolete? Is it not outside of time?

R - Yes, it is outside of time. But there is much more. How can a Truth of the *Upaniṣads*, if it is really such, ever be considered out of date? Does Truth change with the seasons? What is probably meant is that what changes is its *adaptation*. We agree with that: it is clear that Truth itself must be "clothed" according to the literary conventions of the period in which it reveals itself. From this point of view, we can say that every now and then the

Tradition changes appearance and form, but the Truth it contains is always the same, and cannot but be the same; it would otherwise be a simple opinion.[1]

---

[1] See the chapter "Unity of Tradition," in Raphael, *Tat tvam asi*, *op. cit.*

NAME, FORM AND VĀSANĀ

Questioner - Did Raphael have a *guru*?

Raphael - Certainly.

— (same questioner) Can you tell me his name?

R - This is the point: name and form. By always seeking names and forms, we lose sight of that reality that is *Brahman*.

— Unfortunately, I always think in human terms.

R - *Brahman* is capable of manifesting itself in countless ways, not necessarily in a specific form or in one known to us.

— But without a *guru*, how can one escape ignorance? Without a guide, at least at the beginning, how can one find the right way? One might get lost.

R - I think you are right.

— Why don't you act as my guide then?

R - Because you already have a guide.

— I'm sorry to contradict you, but I have no guide.

R - Why do you say this if your most infallible guide is inside of you?

— Won't you show me the way to seek this inner guide?

R - You have simply to learn how to look inside yourself. You have only to question yourself. You have only to recognize yourself as *ātman*.

— But why don't you give me something to help me remove my ignorance? I think this way would be easier than the other.

R - I am already inside you. Raphael is you yourself. We are all Raphael. To ask Raphael something means to ask it of ourselves. Raphael is a state of consciousness.

— Sometimes I ask, but I get no answer. Why?

R - Perhaps because you don't know how to ask. Who is it who asks something?

— It's always I who ask.

R - Whoever asks, wants. One who asks in order to have something does so because he doesn't have it.

— Exactly. I am asking for Knowledge, the solution to my problems. If I didn't have these problems, I wouldn't ask.

R - If he who seeks Knowledge does not have it within himself, he cannot expect to find it outside himself. Knowledge is not a tuber to be picked and eaten. One cannot have what does not pertain to one's own nature.

— What must I do? I am ignorant; I ask you for Knowledge and you refer me back to my ignorance?

R - If your nature is characterized only by *avidyā*-ignorance, you must resign yourself to it. There cannot even be contradiction in such ignorance, and I am amazed that you ask something that does not even belong to your nature.

— I realize that my nature is not ignorance alone, but it is also Knowledge and even Beatitude. I am convinced of this and not only because of faith.

R - Now things change and become simple. If, until today, you have evoked and externalized ignorance, now you must *evoke* and unveil Knowledge.

— This is the problem. How can I evoke Knowledge?

R - I might ask you: how did you evoke ignorance?

— But does Raphael want or not want to help me in my *sādhanā*? I would like a precise answer.

R - Is it possible that your nature, your true essence, refuses to reveal itself? I don't think so. Perhaps it is your ego that fails to comprehend or that is unable to question itself.

— But if my ego is full of ignorance, what definite answer can it give me?

R - This is the right way. The ego is ignorance, while the Self is Knowledge; therefore you must find the Self.
  The Self is Being, Intelligence and Fullness.

— How can I find the Self? The question keeps coming up, as you can see.

R - By dying to ignorance. But how can you die to ignorance if ignorance is always chattering and chasing its own tail? No proper or adequate answer can come from an ego that is ignorant. If one wishes to stand still while he is walking, what must he do?

— Halt, stand still and stop walking.

R - Very well. Now why not stand still? Why not oblige your mind-ignorance to be silent?
  Whoever is still is supremely sovereign. He has reached the end of the journey; he has re-embraced himself as Essence-without-a-second.
  The Reality is silence. Silence is the hub of the wheel, the resolution of polarities, the imperturbability that transcends "heaven" and "earth"; it is peace in the void, the harmony of motionless unity.

— I comprehend that one who is walking and wishes to walk no longer must stop, but when I find myself in silence, my consciousness feels uneasy, at times frustrated. It's as if it were lacking something, and so it hurries to produce movement; it is even afraid of silence.

You see, it seems to me that the awareness of ego and the mind, when lacking motion, suffer.

R - Quite so, this is all true. Besides, movement, becoming and process always require motion and becoming.

If you force the ego into silence, it is inevitable that it will suffer on account of this. By instinct, it recognizes that silence represents its death, and therefore it employs all its resources to eliminate it. The "slowing down" of psychic motion must take place gradually; we cannot stop suddenly, even though in theory this is possible.

If we are able to overcome the ego's force of inertia (*tamas*) of the *guṇas*, we shall enjoy quiet, calmness and silence. But we must keep firmly in mind that the empirical ego will desperately seek to nourish itself. When you have managed to remain in silence for half a day or so, you will notice that afterwards the ego-mind will become more agitated and increasingly demanding; apparently, having intuited its end, it attempts to recover and makes a greater effort to get its breath back. If you do not maintain a firm attitude when faced with the despair of one who is dying, you may be dragged down by it. To give in or become sentimental can prove fatal. Some people, although they seek to get rid of their ego, in actual fact love it.

The paradox is this: we are so full of conflict-motion that we have lost the habit of tasting beatitude. As things

stand at present, I would go as far as saying we are
unprepared to taste beatitude; some even are unable, and
others create complexes for themselves. One may even go
so far as to refuse one's own nature in order to accept
the second conflictual nature one has artificially created.
In brief, we are so attached to the surrogate as to refuse
the pure product.

Q - But where is this psychic strength coming from,
this energy that asks for sensorial experience?

R - It is the accumulated strength of a million yes-
terdays. It is stored, solidified energy, an energy that,
qualified by now, insists upon being listened to, taken
into consideration and expressed. It is the *vāsanās*, the
samskāras, the "thought trends" that have made an impression upon our *substance* and given it a certain impetus,
a certain pace. Observe your psychic comings and goings,
and find out whether this is so.

The greatest joy that can derive from Knowledge is
that of realizing that we can resolve and defeat our mental
fabrications, our energetic tendencies, that is, those pathways that have led us into a blind alley. From this stems
awareness of having to slow down that motion, devoid of
purpose, that we have stamped in time, and that we now
wish to stop in order to recover our tranquillity, our joy
without objects.

Silence is the end of motion, the end of the journey,
the end of conflict and pain. Whosoever wishes to achieve
silence without putting a stop to his own "proceeding" is
like a person who, while wishing to remain silent, continues to speak.

There are those who are not at all qualified to stop; their unconscious motivation, rather than coming to a halt, simply seeks a change of direction or of movement on the horizontal plane.

It is necessary to comprehend whether one is ready to stop in order *to be* or whether one really only needs to change one's life pattern.

Q - I am filled with remorse because of a wrong deed; speaking in religious terms, I might say I have sinned. How can I escape this remorse?

R - What do you mean by sin?

— To break a commandment, go against morality, against a law.

R - If you put your finger in the fire, it burns because a physical law has been broken. We can say that one pays the price. What must you do in order to break this law no longer and avoid paying the consequences?

— I shouldn't put my finger in the fire again. This seems to be the right solution.

R - So, you'll agree that this solution is the only thing worth considering, won't you?

— I do.

R - Then, why do you emphasize *remorse* for having done something?

If sinful action means going against the universal Law, you should try to enter into proper accord with the law. Ethics means acting properly; ethics means living according to the Principle.

Q - Once you said that to live in harmony and in innocence we must eliminate our reactions. But our lives express themselves above all by means of reactions; besides, a person devoid of reactions seems dead to me.

R - The crystallized, reacting world is a construction of the ego-phantom; now, if we knock it down, we can create a new mode of being.[1] Amid the ashes of our incompleteness, we may unveil innocent Beauty, which is neither complication nor heterogeneousness, but *simplicity.* In the world of Beauty, which is commensurate with the Principle, there is no pride, possessiveness, greed, envy, deception and vanity. Human conflict is born because it is motivated by these qualifications. Whoever vanquishes them will be reconciled, harmonized, simplified and innocent.

Q - If I am able to live without being pressured by the subconscious, therefore by the world of reactions, do I place myself within the immediate present? Do I live in a state where there are no existential problems?

R - Yes, certainly. If we observe our (mental, emotional, sexual) action, we will discover that we never act

---

[1] See the chapters relating to the birth and solution of the coagulates in Raphael, *Beyond the Illusion of the Ego: Synthesis of a Realizative Process* (New York: Aurea Vidyā, 2001).

innocently, but rather our actions are always motivated by emotional pleasure-pain memories and by pre-existing mental *conceptualizations*. What we choose to eat is determined by the experience of attraction-repulsion and by image-forms created over time.

When we eat an orange, we simply repeat a mechanical, memorized action. To eat an orange in the *present* means to be free from the orange image-form of the past and also from possible expectations we may obtain from it. To be aware, deeply attentive or watchful during the act of peeling an orange, dividing it up, chewing it and finally perceiving its fragrance or its *qualitative vibration* means being in harmony with the orange, with that particular orange and no other, without seeking comparisons, without conceptualizing perception and without desiring anything from it.

— Can the same be said of sex?

R - Yes. In sex, action is not innocent because it is motivated by image-forms that not only determine the initial action, but also the entire process.[1]

In sexual union, it is not two *jīvas* who encounter each other, love each other and donate themselves to one another. Those who meet and who offer themselves to each other are two image-forms, the outcome of the conceptualization of a relationship, a partner or the mode of action itself, and so on. They are not even two bodies.

---

[1] See the chapter "Solution of the Energy Complex," in Raphael, *Which Democracy?, op. cit.*

— Here, too, it would be necessary to forget the past and expectations for the future, wouldn't it?

R - The act, weighed down by past conditioning, is never experienced in the present. In general, the past or the future is transposed into the present. That is, the act or the union is carried out by the subconscious—which is crystallized psychic accumulation—not by *consciousness* that has awakened to the experience of the present moment.

Some people no longer know if the impulse to unite derives from the rhythm of life or from the psychic image-form that presses on, seeking gratification.

For example, some people eat because they are compelled by psychic restlessness, nervousness or by a psychic urge, rather that by a physical need for food.

Sex expressed in harmony with vital rhythm is neither harmful to, nor does it prevent, *sādhanā* itself, especially that pertaining to the first level of ascent (the first two degrees of the *āśramas*, those of the student and head of household). It may become an obstacle when the form-image of sex acts within the psychic space; this is a monster that continually saps blood and energy to the detriment both of the *sādhanā* and peace of mind. Some are obsessed not by sexuality in itself but by what is an imagined, psychic and mental sexuality.

It is necessary, therefore, to distinguish between a precise instance of polar *creativity* and a sexual, pleasure-seeking impulse born of mere mental form-images.

Humanity, unfortunately, has lost many things inherent in the polar act; it has lost:

1. The rhythms;

2. The proper attitude or approach to union;

3. The appropriate operative modalities during union;

4. A proper comprehension of the body, of the forms and focal points to which the body responds;

5. The correct technique for the conservation and utilization of energy (this concerns male polarity in particular);

6. The proper use of the temporal relationship: initial stimulus, growth, maturation and accomplishment;

7. A contemplative attitude toward the act in itself, toward the complementary polarity as *jīva*-soul and finally toward the body itself.

Polar union, deprived of all these factors, becomes simple habitual discharge of compressed physical energy or gratification of sensory pleasure; from this stems the need to *possess* the object of desire. Today, sex is the fruit of mere emotional, passionate desire and not of joyful and innocent *creative expression*. Sex is the symbol of a higher, universal reality; and as such, it is a sacred act, a rite that replicates the *Puruṣa-Prakṛti* Sacrifice.

— I realize that in actual fact we seek to gratify the image-form. The encounter is not between two souls but between two small or large phantoms, depending on circumstances, seeking compensation, each trying to steal pleasure from the other. But to change things, a certain teaching is necessary. In fact, seen from this point of view, I think that it must be a teaching.

R - In fact it is, and like all teachings, it is not easy to follow, although everybody feels ready for it. Unfortunately, we have to stress that many seek mere psychic pleasure, not ritual polar union; pleasure can be an innocent consequence, an effect.

Q - But can sex not be totally surpassed?

R - Yes. What we have just spoken about concerns certain levels; not only that, but it may be taken into consideration by those who are young or middle-aged. There is no need to remind you that sex is dependence, and for those who seek liberation, all dependence is enslaving. Besides, in the metaphysical dimension, there is no sex. Sex, at whatever level or within whatever dimension it may express itself, is polarity, and polarity lives and thrives upon the relative, manifest plane.

Q - Can an individual offer himself without feeling anything?

R - I don't understand.

— Is it possible to offer oneself as a pure act of donation?

R - Yes, naturally. I think, however, that this is more typical of women, and men are not usually capable of dwelling adequately upon such a deed.

Q - Can one say that there is a Traditional view as far as sex is concerned?

R - Yes. There is a Traditional approach to sex, which does not involve consumerism, gratification for one's own sake, procreation without awareness, possessiveness or physiological satisfaction.[1]

The approach begins in the dimension of *buddhi* and can direct itself downwards, seeking to achieve fusion with the manasic and pranic bodies, with the dense body acting as support. This may be considered as a "launching pad" from which to take flight upwards like a rubber ball, which, having been thrown into the air, uses the earth as the support from which to bounce back upwards.

We can say that at certain levels polar union may take the form of meditation, but we are speaking of *union,* not of copulation for the gratification of selfish pleasure for its own sake. The human race has used and continues to use sex without achieving psycho-physical harmony, and this means that there is something missing on the plane of sexual behavior.

Q - I tried to experience mental silence, and when I achieved it, I was afraid: I immediately plunged back into thought and tried to become aware of my sensory ego. Am I not ready, perhaps?

R - To vanquish the empirical ego's spirit of preservation requires comprehension, maturation and courage. For some, this requires more than a day. However, there is no reason to become discouraged. At the beginning, the child jumping into the water is afraid of drowning; then, with

---

[1] See Raphael, *The Science of Love: From the Desire of the Senses to the Intellect of Love* (New York: Aurea Vidyā, 2010).

intelligence and comprehension, he acquires courage and confidence to the point of allowing himself to be cradled and carried by the water. You must also consider that the psychological ego has no absolute reality; it changes from one moment to the next without our noticing it.

Q - There are no rulers or men of culture who do not preach morals, but morals, however much preached, are not put into practice by anybody. Why?

R - For the simple reason that they speak of something that does not exist. If I tell you to follow a bird's footsteps, you cannot, because birds leave no footsteps.

— Sorry, I don't understand; I am rather perplexed. Could you explain yourself better, please?

R - There is only one Ethic, and it is the one commensurate to and in accord with the Principle.[1] Today's view, generally speaking, has no place for the Principle. Therefore we can deduce that the ethic being pursued is not the real Ethic, but a simple question of moral custom, mere sentiment or the mood of the historical moment, a state of mind that may even be aggressive. Thus we have an aggressive, institutionalized morality.

In a society where sentimental humanism triumphs, morality simply becomes defense of the postulates that emerge from the contingent reality, defense of a *fashion*, be it in literature, commerce, clothing, politics, etc.

---

[1] See the chapter "The Last Freedom," in Raphael, *Which Democracy?, op. cit.*

— How can we establish the true Ethic?

R - First of all, by recognizing that there is something greater than the human being as such. The individual should abandon his anthropocentric position; but this requires great humility and great ability to broaden one's consciousness.

Q - If the Hindu doctrine holds that all is *līlā*, that is, play, I wonder what sense there is in speaking of ethical action in agreement with the Principle.
What kind of proper action can there be in this fantastic and senseless game?

R - Allow me to say that perhaps you haven't really understood the meaning of the term *līlā*.

— I hope so; otherwise, certain conclusions will become absurd.

R - In Sanskrit, *līlā* means "play," action performed as a game. This kind of divine play-action is the opposite of the astute and predetermined action of the interested individual.

The action of an individual is:

1. Motivated by selfish interest;

2. Turned toward gratification and sensory satisfaction;

3. Directed toward the expansion and assertion of the ego;

4. Characterized by dramatic sense.

Divine action is like child's play: it does not stem from any particular selfish interest, is not aimed at gratifying any subconscious need and does not seek to glorify itself to the detriment of others. We might say that this kind of action is *innocent*, action without action, a state of being without desires, pure, simple action. It is life for life's sake, without any kind of superimposition.

The action conformed to the Principle is spontaneous; it does not involve any effort, any tension, any conflict. It is *līlā*, innocent play like the flight of a swallow.

Human life is a continuous fight of overpowering, of tension, of brutishness because the right kind of innocent, non-dramatic action, action that is utilized when healthy play or pure sport is experienced, is not realized. Compare some of these thoughts to what was said about sex, and you will draw other profitable conclusions.

VIBRATING LIFE

Questioner - Sometimes you have interpreted instinct, emotion and thought in terms of vibration; that is, you have considered the individuality as existential rhythm with its own musical scale. Now I would like to go more deeply into this vision and seek points of reflection. I would like to ask our friends here not to wander off the theme, if possible. I believe that this dialogue may be of use to everybody.

Raphael - On the plane of the manifest, there is no thing or being that does not express rhythm, vibration or sound. Even though many vibrations are not perceived, they nevertheless exist. Thus, the individual, as well as all other beings, vibrates and resounds; those who have a particular *sensitivity* are able to perceive this sound-rhythm.

It is necessary, however, to go a little further and say that, in turn, all vibrations express a particular *tone* or quality. Life is the result of two factors: number and tone. A bird with its sound vibrations expresses a tonal *quality*, a mood, a living, a being. So also a flower with its own vibration or luminous spectrum expresses an influence, a quality.

This implies that if we comprehend, besides the vibration-number, the expressive quality, we can *communicate* with universal life. Our metallization and individualization have forced us into isolation and incommunicability; for us, the luminous-sounding book of life remains closed.

In general, our approach to life occurs only in terms of "counting," quantification, computation and classification. Let us open this book on botany at the word "Orchids" and read what it says:

"Family of monocotyledonous plants, of the microsperm order. The flowers are zygomorphic, trimerous, homochlamydeous or heterochlamydeous, with an uneven anterior frame called a labellum. Of the three stamens, two abort and the remaining one unites with the pistil forming the gymnostemium. The anther is bilocular and contains the conglomerated pollen forming 2, 4 or 8 pollinia. The lower tricarpellary ovary, with its three parietal placentas, originates a capsule containing numerous tiny seeds, with undifferentiated or slightly differentiated embryo, devoid of albumen."

Let us stop here and intuit the rest.

Thanks to this numbering, classifying and invention of words, one believes one knows the orchid. Let us say that not only does one not know it, but one does not even comprehend what this kind of classification means.

Whoever really wants to know the orchid must *feel* it vibrate, listen to it and be *sensitive* to its expressive tones, because a plant is not a dead being, an inexpressive void or an illusion, but a life that reveals itself through numbers and tones.

We are accustomed to getting to know data through sight, having shut our inner hearing-sensitivity. Without inner hearing, we can never communicate with life, grasp its message or comprehend its language. The human being has become a mere mechanical "accountant," always intent on counting, adding, multiplying and classifying.

— (same questioner) Does this classifying and naming of the various forms have some kind of validity of its own?

R - In actual fact, it does have a relative validity. It is not important to give things names, although at certain levels this can prove useful. When we have simply classified or named things, we find we are still at the point of departure. We live with other *lives* in nature and yet, although we describe and classify them, we neither understand nor *listen* to them.

— This leads me to the supposition that a form is music. Is life therefore music?

R - One might say yes. It is sound and also color, whereby one must be *sensitive* toward the one and the other in order to be able to *communicate* with life. This appears clear upon the more *subtle* planes of manifestation.

Q - I think that such an approach to the world of things or forms, being new, requires appropriate preparation. One would have to reinterpret completely one's conception of relationship with it.

R - This view is not new; it is as old as Being because it comes from life itself. Let us say that what is new, but also deviating, is the conception that seeks to name and classify without communicating and comprehending. This *novelty*, unfortunately, has interrupted our *dia-*

logue with life, has isolated us and caused us to consider ourselves absolute, with the right of life and death in the environment around us.

— What, for example, gives harmony to the vegetable kingdom?

R - The variety of its luminous sounds. Depending on its vegetation, a field may produce discordant or assonant music. Let us say that, on the whole, it exhibits its expressive tonal note. Thus one must know which plant-sounds to sow in order to create musical-vegetable harmony.

Harmony comes from the ensemble, rather, from the unity, from the whole, from the totality. The whole, as is now well known, is more than the sum of the parts. The parts are simply quantity, but the whole is also quality. So, a set of musical notes creates a chord, but this is more than the algebraic sum of the notes.

It is well to repeat that each vibration or tonal number emanates a quality or a tonal value; that is, the rhythm vibration represented by a rose emits a qualitative effect. With our five psycho-physical senses, we perceive the rhythm-quantity (tonal number), and with the *sensitivity* of our soul or the soul's subtle senses, we perceive the quality or the tonal value of the rose-rhythm.

From this point of view, we can *hear* and *evaluate* all that surrounds us; we can perceive harmony or the music-quality of universal life, and we can hear and live, as Hans Kayser has demonstrated, the "music of the spheres." Each being expresses vibratory, qualitative tones, which, taken together, represent the "musical tone" or the harmony of that being.

To comprehend a being, of whatever degree or size it may be, we must develop our "inner ear," our inner sensitivity, which is not emotion or feeling, but something much more. To appreciate the tonal value of a score by Beethoven, simple sentimental emotion is not enough.

Q - I presume that this is also true as far as relations between individuals are concerned. Humanity fails to comprehend itself because it has not developed this special "inner hearing"?

R - Yes, in a certain way. When we see a child, however much we may know about the numerical structure of his glands, his metabolism, his teeth and so on, if we are devoid of that type of *hearing*, we may never comprehend that child. To communicate with him, we require a kind of sensitivity that transcends mere physiological relationships.

If a child smiles, he expresses a particular qualified rhythm vibration that fills the surrounding space (like the perfume of a flower wafting through the air); whoever is endowed with "inner hearing" may tune into this rhythm and *comprehend* the child's state of mind. But if we read a book about human physiology and consult the term "smile," or, better, "laughter," we may read something like this: laughter deeply modifies the breathing rhythm and facial expression because of the drawing back of the lips and the closure of the eyelids. It causes muscular contraction, and so on. All these quantitative, peripheral details fail to enable us to comprehend the childish soul that expresses itself through the smile.

The plant also has its smiles and its weeping, its pleasure and pain, and if one does not have its kind of

hearing, one fails to grasp the most significant aspect of
the reality that the plant expresses.

Q - Might we call sound the vehicle of quality? Yet
a sound that does not express anything is simply a set
of lifeless notes.

R - Yes. We might say that sound is the *support*
through which quality expresses itself.

In general, science classifies sound but is not interested
in quality. This implies that it neglects the deep, expressive and vital side of sound, that is, it neglects the soul.

Q - Is quality the final aspect of sound manifestation?

R - Behind quality there is Life or Being. In order to
comprehend this concept better, we might say that *Being*
expresses its *tonal quality* by means of *form-number-sound*.
Therefore, we have life, quality and form, but these three
aspects are not distinct and separate; they are a unitarian
triad. The quality is the basic Tone or the fundamental
qualitative Note of Being-life. This Note obviously develops
harmonics that are the countless expressive modalities of
life itself; thus the individual is a particular harmonic of
the fundamental Note of Being-life.

Q - Can one say it is an emanation of the God Person?

R - Yes. *Īśvara*, for example, represents the fundamental Note of all manifest and non-manifest existence
but is only one of the infinite Notes of *nirguṇa Brahman*.
All the harmonics (forms of life) are simply undertones,

and the different modulations of life all have that Note as their essence, and the fundamental Note cannot reveal other than these particular harmonics.

Q - Could you illustrate this through an example, please?

R - Lines, planes and volumes are all simply harmonics of the point. The point, which is the fundamental note, cannot develop other than lines, planes and volumes; therefore, every geometric figure goes back to the point, which is the basis from which it stemmed. In geometry, the point is the prime determination and, as such, has its own limits. It is, therefore, determined and qualified, even though it is considered to have no dimension: this is the idea of *saguṇa Brahman* as first determination of universal life, however unlimited.

The geometric point, therefore, has its own particular *vibration* and its own particular *quality,* which make it what it is.

Thus *Īśvara,* as macrocosmic Point, is a vibration (sound) with a particular *quality* (tone). If we keep this principle in mind, then all beings, as harmonics of the fundamental Note, also have a particular vibration (sound) and a certain quality (tone). If we can recognize the sound-tone of each being, we communicate with life, resound with life and become living *music.* But in order to do this, we require two instruments: that provided by our external senses and that which the inner senses give us, senses that we all have but that, unfortunately, we do not use.

When, for example, we listen to a piece of music, we use our outer hearing, which we need in order to perceive the sound, and we use our inner hearing or the sensitiv-

ity of our consciousness to *appreciate*, evaluate and communicate with the Harmony that sound seeks to express.
That is, we avail of a certain inner sense to perceive the
quality of that piece of music.

Thus, in front of a tree, we have to use our sight
to perceive the form-tree, and our inner hearing, or the
sensitivity of our consciousness, to perceive the quality
expressed by that form.

Quality and form may be related to *tonal value* and
to *tonal number.*

Q - If I am not mistaken, is this inner faculty resolving the problem of quality-quantity duality? In other words,
isn't it able to solve the dualism of life?

R - Yes. The link between number and tone, or between form and quality, is inner hearing. One must recognize the fact that this faculty is not simple "subjective
evaluation" or emotional perception; furthermore, it cannot
be denied. And yet we might ask ourselves: who would
dare disown the existence of the inner sense that gives us
the opportunity to interpret music, literature, sculpture and
even the laws of science?

— If some do not take it into consideration, this is
because it cannot be seen by the physical eyes.

R - But neither is the intelligence, or what we call such,
visible with the physical eyes, and yet it cannot be denied.

— I think that some things can be taken into consideration only when the individual frees himself from physical-corporeal conditioning.

R - I think so too. It is undeniable that many things exist and are accepted, even though they cannot be perceived by the five senses. We experience the inner faculty every day, just as we experience intelligence and pleasure-pain.

— If we could put these tonal numbers and values down on paper, would we obtain a musical score?

R - Yes. Even quality can have a scale of values.

— And if this score were played by a special instrument, could the specific tree, of which the score is an X-ray, respond?

R - Yes. Let's say there is perfect communion, perfect harmony, and that the distance, or the split, between number and quality would be filled and transcended.

Q - From this point of view, could there be a new science?

R - Yes, the "Science of Harmony," of which Pythagoras was the supreme Master.[1]

---

[1] See Raphael, *The Threefold Pathway of Fire*, especially the chapter "All-Pervading Fire: Realization according to Love of Beauty," *op cit.*

— From what we have said, I must deduce that each of nature's realms has its own tonal note and its own number-sound. Have the sub-human realms lower notes than ours?

R - Each realm of life, or each life mode, has its own form-quality, thus a tone and a number that can differentiate itself within the ambit of the variety of its own species.

The four realms of life that we perceive have a range of sound-tones that move in a crescendo from the mineral to the human. Beyond the human, the tone-numbers are so high that the human senses cannot perceive them. However, we must add that the human being is also endowed with subtler and more vibrant body-vehicles with which he could see, hear and perceive very well.

Q - Can we say that the fundamental Note of the natural realm is the archetype of the entire realm?

R - Yes, if we choose the language of philosophy. According to Plato, every realm of life or life mode is an Idea, and to relate to such an Idea means being in harmony with the realm it expresses.[1] Naturally, in order to do this, we must hear, with our inner hearing, the tone-quality or what the Idea incarnates.

— We know that human individuality expresses itself by means of instinct, emotion and thought. Now, from what we have said, individuality must represent a number and a tone. Does it, therefore, also constitute a fundamental note?

---

[1] See the chapter "Platonic Dualism?" in Raphael, *Initiation into the Philosophy of Plato*, op. cit.

R - Yes. Human individuality is always a particular harmonic of the primary or principial Note of Being. We can say, for example, that a disciple, in time-space, vibrated and intoned that harmony and then surpassed it, transcending it to the point where it no longer constitutes his expressive *music* because he has changed his note.

An instinct, an emotion and a thought are nothing but particular states of vibration through which one tries to express qualified tones. If one expresses himself or strikes a tone of affection, his vibrations may be heard or perceived by a sensitive psychic string. A thought is represented by vibrating waves, which may be perceived by an individual even very far from the emitting source. However, we should mention that the note of individuality is a degraded note, its music out of tune and discordant.

Q - If one wishes to go deeper into this, how does this sound process work?

R - We haven't very much time. What we have said is a mere fraction of a vast and deep science.

In order to answer this question very briefly, we can say that the being, by means of a note (number-tone), sets in motion *ākāśa*, the first element on the existential plane upon which it intends operating, which responds by molding itself on that note.

Being is the great Musician who, on his *noûs-logos* keyboard, plays the notes of harmony, modelling substance or *ākāśa*. From this act, two effects spring: number-harmonics and tonal quality. The human individual repeats the event and the process: using the keyboard of his *logos*-intellect, he plays some notes and the *ākāśa*-substance molds itself. Emotions or thoughts are the effects of an impulse or purpose of the human demiurge or musician; they are, as we said already, vibratory states that express quality. Unfortunately, humanity, with its keyboard of *logos*-intellect, plays discordant, disharmonic notes, thus producing, if we can express ourselves in these terms, bad music. In fact, within the various human harmonics, there is no accord, no harmony, no music that exalts and inebriates. And yet it is always up to the individual human being and not up to others to learn his own trade as musician of life.

— What should man do?

R - He should recognize two facts: that he is a demiurge and molder of events and destinies, and that he can train the string of consciousness in such a manner as to produce harmonious chords.[1]

Humanity is composed of tone-deaf players; furthermore, each player wants to be a soloist. Humanity is in a state of conflict because it wants to be. The human being transforms this world into a field of suffering and pain because he wants to. Nobody prevents him from changing *note* and attuning himself to the Harmony of the spheres.

The individual often blames the Divinity for his poor use of the instrument, but this means he is trying to shirk his own responsibility. It is the capricious and childlike individual who does not wish to grow up and recognize the fact that, after all is said and done, he too is a Musi-

---

[1] See the chapter "Platonism and Vedānta," in Raphael, *Initiation into the Philosophy of Plato, op. cit.*

cian, a molder of mortifying or exalting music, according to whichever he chooses to play.

— Is this because he does not wish to perfect his instrument?

R - The two possibilities we spoke about before can be achieved: first of all, by means of a deep realization that one is a musician-demiurge; then, by becoming aware that one must educate the tonal *quality* of the string of consciousness. Humanity expresses a tonal quality that does not radiate harmony. Therefore, it must modify or change its *tonal key*; in order to do this, precise and committed direct action is required, that involves modifying something that springs from the very depth of the being. This is why we have always said that only a *transformation of the quality of consciousness* can make humanity better. At this level a note is played that strikes the *ākāśa*, not the outer edge of being, relating it to a new expressive quality. The worst conviction is believing that the world is as it is because that is the way things are: that politics, human relations, etc., are as they are and cannot be modified. The individual rarely says: I am the way I am, what can I do about it? This conviction is, as I was saying, detrimental, not only because it is wrong and false, but also because it does not commit one to change *musical key*. For thousands of years now we have been repeating the same discordant music and doing little to change it. The Tradition carries out, allow me to use the word, a marvellous work because it tries to let humanity comprehend that it must change its note and also offers it the means by which to change it.

Jesus proposed sounding the *note of love* to create accord and harmony. Buddha said that the note of desire leads, alas, to conflict and pain. Śaṅkara highlighted the fact that the world of phenomena is not the absolute constant or the absolute Note, and made us comprehend that man's greatest struggles are derived from his taking the relative for the absolute, the fleeting for the permanent, or, in other words, the snake for the rope. But, unfortunately, the darkness or discordant notes, having crystallized, fail to comprehend the Harmony of the spheres and refuse it with scorn and pride. Today we are producing only new bodies (it is believed that we shall soon reach the startling number of over 12 billion individuals); that is, we are increasing only the *volume* of the sound-vibration, but we are doing very little to produce a better *quality* of humanity. We cannot solve the problem simply by raising the level of the volume or the energetic intensity of the sound; indeed, we only make it more complicated. In this field too, if we do not apply a volume *regulator* (order-giver *logos*), the problem may dilate and expand to such an extent as to suffocate the single notes and the very structure of life.

Q - At the social level, does this harmony manifest itself through the structure of the *social orders*?

R - To great extent, yes, but we already spoke about this on another occasion, and there is no need to take on the subject again.[1]

---

[1] See the chapter "Social Orders," in Raphael, *Which Democracy?*, op. cit.

ASPARŚAYOGA

Questioner - *Asparśayoga* is called the *yoga* without relations, without props, supports or contacts of any kind. If this definition is exact, I wish to ask: does not the *yogi* who undertakes *sādhanā* in order to reach liberation place himself upon a plane of contact with something that is represented, in this case, by liberation itself? What I mean is, does liberation itself not represent a support?

Raphael - Yes, this is true. When we think of liberation, of knowledge, of beatitude, we nearly always think of something outside of ourselves, something to be *obtained, had* or *possessed.*

And so we turn liberation into an idea of "objective reality," a distant datum to be reached or achieved. From this point of view, the ego, by objectifying liberation, is in an alienated position, and because it is unable to possess what is outside of itself, it is frustrated.

We can say that when the ego operates in this manner, liberation represents a support with which the ego plays, and which must be abandoned if one wishes to free consciousness from the *concept* of liberation. But it is only a game that sooner or later will have to be left behind if one wishes for consciousness to be freed from the *concept* of liberation. With *Asparśayoga,* gradually all supports fall away until the utmost conclusion: "The supreme truth is this: there is neither birth nor dissolution, nor aspirant to liberation nor liberated, nor anyone in bondage."[1]

Q - You have often said that one must not act as a missionary, need not convince anyone to follow the Doctrine and must not seek disciples; but wasn't *Asparśavāda* meant to be offered to everyone?

R - Yes, *Asparśavāda* is available to everyone. But what we require is neither to force, nor to propose a branch of the Doctrine opposing someone else, nor to want to redeem someone at all costs because one thinks one is endowed with a special *dharma*.

— What should we deduce from what you are saying?

R - That everything is in its proper place, in accordance with the motivating causes and the qualifications of the beings involved in the process.

— Does this mean that each one must live for himself?

R - This is not the problem, nor do we agree with this principle. However, it is necessary to recognize that in the entirety of life there are numerous pathways that, in time-space, may all be valid. In other words, *saṁsāra,* with its unlimited expressions, and *nirvāṇa* are precise modes of consciousness, and each being may choose one or the other, depending upon one's line of thought: "One becomes what one thinks." There is no reason to want to

---

[1] *Kārikā* 32, Chapter II, Gauḍapāda, *Māṇḍūkyakārikā, op. cit.*

uproot a being from a certain pathway, especially if this way is congenial to him.

If we claim that our pathway is better than another and even convince others to pursue it, we would place ourselves in an irrational opposition. *Vidyā* and *avidyā* are two pathways that may equally be followed, depending upon what one wants.

— But *avidyā* leads to pain and slavery.

R - That's another question. It is clear that every pathway has its own existential modality, produces certain effects, causes particular events, and so on. To put one's finger in the fire is a particular experience, although painful, but if someone wants to try it, he is free to do so. Nobody can prevent him. This is free will.

However, if a person is mature, tired or aware of the inanity of following certain pathways, then we are happy to let him know that it is possible to emerge from this stagnant condition. One can have a fruitful dialogue only with someone who is ready to receive the new way. Besides, the *Gītā* states that one must not disturb those who are content to follow a certain path.

Q - There is an almost innate tendency that urges us to give others what often they do not want. But this also occurs at the political-social level; in fact, they oblige you to act or to follow a certain ideology because, again according to them, this is for your own good.

R - The history of humanity is nearly always characterized by a *desire* to give others what often one neither has, nor has been asked for. The individual is restless and hyperactive. As long as he is busy within his own ambit, one can accept him; but when he tries to impose his way of life on others, things become complicated.

Q - But didn't Jesus, for example, come to save others?

R - Jesus came to bring light into the darkness of selfishness. His way is one of redemption, and whoever so wishes can simply follow it.
He did not come to judge the other ways, to condemn or to impose his own view forcefully. If in time this has occurred, it is because of his fanatical followers who failed to understand his message of Love. Besides, he said not to give pearls to those unable to appreciate them, nor sacred things to the dogs. Anyway, the "Sermon on the Mount" is there. Whosoever wishes to, may put it into practice, live by it and incarnate it. There is no need to ask anyone's permission.

Q - For quite some time I have understood what has just been said and I think that it is deeply just.
Each of us, because of our free will, can follow the pathway of *māyā* or that of *Brahman*. Having chosen the latter, I wish to ask if with *Asparśa* it is necessary to cast off every egoistic reference; for example, whether even *nirvāṇa* itself must be transcended. Although we have already spoken about this, I wish to underline this point.

R - There is a *sūfi* proverb that goes more or less like this: paradise is a prison for the sage, just as the world of *saṁsāra* is a prison for the simple believer.

— To deprive the ego of all it possesses produces a serious form of neurosis, which must be kept in mind if we don't want our *sādhanā* to end in failure. *Bhakti*, by giving the neophyte the support of an *ideal* or of a God Person, is less liable to lead one into frustrating attitudes.

R - First of all, it is essential to underline the fact that every neophyte is driven by a predominance of *guṇas*, in other words, by his own vocation. In order to handle the problem of man's vocations, the Tradition offers different pathways that may prove useful at the appropriate moment. Furthermore, one must also keep in mind the state of consciousness of the aspirant-disciple when he begins his *sādhanā*. It is inevitable that there must be an examination of the psychological condition, the strength of aspiration, the subconscious obstacles, the karmic limitations, etc., that is, all those things that are a part of the *sādhanā* itself. The individuality cannot be suddenly deprived of all supports, although in theory this is possible, but there is an inevitable necessity to *die* daily to something, to the point of turning the individuality into a simple phantom bent upon itself.

Frustration and neuroses occur because opposition arises between the will of today and that of yesterday, between the awareness of self-determination along a certain line and possible subconscious reactions with different demands. It must also be recognized that where there is precise determination and a stable center of consciousness, the subconscious can be forced. If determination or an operative center of consciousness is lacking, it is better not to confront subconscious resistance directly.

But these aspects of stimulus, process and solution are a part of *sādhanā* and therefore of the disciple-teacher relationship.

Q - In the West it is quite common to dramatize the importance of subconscious processes. Today it is held that all subconscious content must be externalized; otherwise, the ego will never fulfill itself. Therefore, it is necessary to release repressed and removed energies. Is this way of seeing things in contrast to the *yoga* point of view?

R - The problem is vast and serious and cannot be treated fully in a few minutes.

There are some psychologies that interpret the being in its totality as simple individuality composed of thought, feeling and instinct. The ego is the center of coordination. When the ego comes to a decision but is censured by some subconscious content, it cannot express or manifest itself. Thus the problem arises of solving oneself, of freeing and letting emerge the demands without censure and opposition.[1]

A primitive person, by way of example, who lives freely with and in nature, has no psychological problems, while the so-called "civilized" man, who is constricted by moral dogmas of all kinds (family, religion, politics, society, etc.), cannot but feel himself circumscribed, in conflict, in duality, frustrated and neurotic.

---

[1] See the chapter "The Limits of the Mind," in Raphael, *At the Source of Life, op. cit.*

— At this point, it is possible to draw some conclusions: if an individual person expresses himself without moral restrictions and prejudices, he may feel more realized. If he arrives at conscious licentiousness, he may even find himself able to express his ego fully. In other words, whoever lives in absolute licentiousness is realized. Believe me, this perplexes me.

R - We said previously that the problem is extremely complex. Besides, there has been a misunderstanding concerning what has been said.

— Sorry if I insist. I once knew a person who, urged by a need for violence, would have felt realized, according to himself, had he killed someone. But a social restriction prevented him from doing so, or, rather, curbed this inclination of his. What should he have done: given way to instinct and killed?

R - I see we don't comprehend each other. This is not the problem, nor is it what we were aiming at.

Q - I think the question might be posed in a different way.
If a particular kind of psychology considers the individual as mere mind, feeling and instinct, as much as one freely manifests oneself through these attributes, can one be fulfilled and happy?

R - This is a pertinent question; we may now proceed.
Our real problem is exactly this: is the individuality as such, the empirical self as a center of decision, capable

of finding fulfillment and *pax profunda*, even when given the possibility of freely expressing its instincts, sentiments and thoughts in all possible ways?

— There are individuals who seem to be happy to work, eat and copulate. Could their ego have found happiness relative to their particular state of evolution?

R - First of all, we should not take into consideration just a particular individuality as such, but consider whether individuality, as an extensive concept embracing all beings, is capable of finding fulfillment or not. We want to know whether "individual nature" is capable or not of being *pax profunda*.

There are many who are deeply circumscribed and live within their circumference without apparent problems; there are others, on the contrary, who *stupefy* themselves by externalizing thought, feelings and instinct, thus drowning their real existential problems. There are others who create continuous *compensations*, convinced that the problems have been solved or are non-existent. We might use other examples, but we haven't got the time now.

We are interested in knowing whether human individuality in its triple expression is capable of finding beatitude of the heart. We might also consider whether this individuality is capable of expressing true Will, pure Love and right Action.

— If I am not mistaken, should the problem be posed in absolute terms?

R - Let us say so. We must comprehend whether individuality is or is not capable of expressing certain things.

— If individuality had been capable of this, it would have already expressed it. The history of the individual is one of conflict and pain, alas, with the odd pause for peace and psychic tranquillity. As a result, I think that individuality is simply restlessness and neurosis.

Q - (another questioner) But allow me to say that we cannot conceive of a future paradise outside of the circumference of the individual. I cannot believe that an individual is capable of finding happiness in one place and misery and conflict in another; that is, I don't think that the earth can be considered the cause of conflict, and that paradise, as normally imagined, up in the skies, is capable of bestowing happiness.

R - I see what you mean. We never said that life was to be considered a set of watertight compartments or that beings should look elsewhere for what is and *must be* always and everywhere. Either wholeness is inherent to being or being cannot have what its nature does not potentially possess. Therefore, it is not a question of leaving something immediate for some hypothetical and vague future advantage. Keep in mind also that for the *Asparśa* there is the *jīvanmukta*, the "living liberated." This is worthy of reflection.

— In any case, to be fulfilled, the individuality must sacrifice, abandon or reject material well-being in general.

R - Even in this case, it is not a question of *abandoning* or sacrificing something, but of knowing whether a certain possibility, a particular datum or another experience is concretely able to give the individual completeness or not.

— One might ask: if an individual has material well-being, wealth, affection, prestige and so on, can he be complete?

— (a different questioner) I am well-to-do, have a family, have a professional post of responsibility, and yet I am here in an effort to fill gaps that I have recently discovered and recognized.

R - Although your position upon the empirical plane is excellent, why are you not happy?

— For a long time, I was a materialist agreeing in full consciousness with that philosophy. I believed that every other form of philosophy, including that of a spiritual nature, was a source of escapism and a waste of time. Then I went through a crisis of values, both exterior and interior: social, political and so on. The crisis was preceded by a restlessness and lack of satisfaction, which created conflict and anguish in me. I didn't recognize the reasons because, in looking at my situation, I had and still have, as you said, an excellent lifestyle. I had psychoanalytical treatment, but that did not solve the problem. Later, through reading certain things, which before then I had always decidedly rejected, my consciousness began to find a harmony with them, a correspondence to the point of realizing that my crisis was of a vertical nature.

Perhaps I have spoken of too many personal matters that are of no interest to others. I'm sorry, but you see...

R - No, on the contrary. We are here to communicate. If you wish, please speak to us about the present-day position of your consciousness.

— Today I have the precise impression that being is more than a simple body with all its interest in hoarding, more even than affection and the faculty of thinking. Being cannot be fully explained in terms of these relative and contingent factors. I must say that today I strongly reject such a possibility, because I also have seen that money, for example, fails to bring fulfillment, but simply offers one the chance of spending one's brief earthly life more comfortably, of affording certain forms of amusement, that is, of allowing a greater amount of evasion. What I mean is that money is not the yardstick of life, affection or politics.

R - Do you believe, therefore, that individuality in itself, even in the most favorable material circumstances, is incapable of being whole?

— Up until recently I did not think so; I do so today.

R - And so, what can we deduce from this hypothesis? Do the others wish to take part in this dialogue?

Q - May we consider this, that if the individual does not have in himself the possibility of being whole, there are two consequences: rejecting life or turning the gaze toward new and unusual spheres of being, because the triple individuality that we were speaking about earlier cannot constitute the being's totality, but simply represents a part, a periphery, if anything, an accident.

R - If the others agree, we may accept this conclusion. In other words, either we refuse existence, thus favoring suicide, or we must look within the being itself and seek those spheres that are inaccessible to the senses. This is what the Orient, generally speaking, has done. This is what the Philosophy of Being proposes and what *Asparśavāda* postulates.

The being is composed of body, soul and spirit, and only when the three become unity can one find that wholeness and fullness that we spoke of earlier. As long as the individual experiences only a segment of his entire circumference, all he can hope to find is conflict and neurosis.

This quest for supraindividual spheres can be carried out in a manner that is practical, experimental and, I would say, scientific, to use terms we are fond of nowadays.

It is not, therefore, a question of seeking a distant, doubtful, heavenly paradise, or of abstaining from or refusing food or other earthly experiences, nor is it, in other terms, a matter of fleeing from the "material world." It is a question of discovering the true total reality of being, openmindedly, free of preconceptions and deforming passions.

POST MORTEM AND BARDO THÖTRÖL

Questioner - With a group of friends, I would like to ask some questions about the practical attitude to take when faced with certain events during life and after leaving the physical, all within the context of the *Bardo Thötröl*.

Although we are interested in *Asparśavāda,* nonetheless I think that having a practical comprehension of certain acts of the individuality can help us reach the state of consciousness of the *asparśin.*

One question is this: do a first and a second death exist?

Raphael - We think it is very important to understand that there is a *solution* or death, as it is often called, of various vehicles or bodies of manifestation, of which the physical one is the outermost, and a *solution* of the entity called individuality. The latter represents the true death-solution, because with it one achieves liberation or the integration of the incarnated reflection of consciousness with the *ātman.* When one abandons the dense physical or the more internal manasic body, even though one may believe oneself to be *dead,* nevertheless one is not dead. One has simply abandoned *momentarily* one vehicle of expression, because of the law of cycles or of rhythm.

The *Bardo Thötröl* is, above all, a teaching aimed at
transcending individuality and achieving integration with
the "Clear Light of *Dharma*." From this point of view, it
is meant not for the "dead," but for the living.

Q - Thank you for this explanation; I think that the
idea is clearer to us now. I had heard talk of a number
of "deaths" but failed to grasp the meaning.

Now, speaking of the dissolution of vehicles, how does
the retreat from the physical body occur? Are there pre-
established stages according to which the entity performs
the withdrawal from the physical body? If in being born
there are precise sequences of development, I think these
should also exist in the case of death.

R - In order to understand this event more thoroughly,
we need to say that the *jīvātmā* is clothed in five sheaths
or bodies of expression, of relationship or contact with the
gross and subtle objective world. Each body is a window
overlooking the existential plane upon which the *jīvātmā*
operates and experiences.[1]

Each existential plane is a state of consciousness more
than a particular spacial point. It is a vibratory condition
with its own scale of values or wavelengths, and where
each one ends, the one immediately above it begins with
increasingly higher vibrations, and so on.

The physical state in which we find ourselves at the
moment is, therefore, a particular vibratory state that, in

---

[1] For an in-depth treatment of the bodies-sheaths, see *ślokas* 154-
209, in Śaṅkara, *Vivekacūḍāmaṇi*, *op. cit.*, and Raphael's commentary
on *sūtra* 30 of Chapter II of the *Bhagavadgītā*, *op. cit.*

order to be perceived, needs a body of contact correlated to the wavelengths of this particular state. When the individual leaves the physical body, he also abandons the possibility of keeping in contact with its corresponding plane. Now, how does the *withdrawal* of the physical body occur? We consider the term *withdrawal* to be the most appropriate because the *jīvātmā*—or, better, the incarnate reflection of consciousness—simply draws back the double *thread* linked to the physical body, allowing the latter to disintegrate and return to the reservoir of nature from which, after all, it was taken. The *jīvātmā,* at the moment of its incarnation, borrows a number of mineral or chemical *elements* from physical nature's reservoir, which it gives back when it retires to other states of manifestation.

An incarnation is simply *exteriorization* upon a particular plane of existence, while *withdrawal* is characterized by a process of *interiorization* or *abstraction.* It is important to meditate upon these terms because they are capable of revealing to us the mystery of what we, erroneously, usually call "death."

When the withdrawal of the incarnate reflection of consciousness occurs, a number of *cakras* connected with the gross physical body are involved: that of the heart, that of the head and another two minor centers linked with the lungs.

The first *disconnection* regards the thread of consciousness; when this occurs, the being loses contact with the five senses of action, but does not lose the awareness of perceiving, although he is unable to respond because the *grip* on the senses of physical action has loosened, for instance, the one pertaining to the vocal cords. This state is like a daydream in which one perceives but does not have the strength to react.

Next comes the detaching or disconnection of the thread of the two minor lung centers. This disconnection may be reactivated in particular conditions by bringing mechanical action to bear upon the lungs.

Finally, the thread of life anchored in the heart is disconnected. At this point the total and definitive abstraction of the physical body occurs.

This withdrawal process takes place in pre-established stages, and if it is a *yogi* withdrawing, these phases can be actuated in a conscious, deliberate way and more rapidly.

With the abstraction process there is no pain, struggle or suffering; some find themselves in their next body, the *prāṇa* body, without any perception of having been sundered from their previous physical form.

Q - Once the physical clothing has been laid down, does one find oneself in one's *prāṇa* attire? And for how long?

R - Yes. The other body of expression is the *prāṇa* one (*prāṇamayakośa*).

At this point it would be useful to clarify one thing. The *prāṇa* body, although it also belongs to the gross physical sphere, is its quintessence. It is, at least in the sense given to it here, the first element, the *materia prima*, from which other grosser elements (*bhūtas*) are born: air (*vāyu*), fire (*tejas*), water (*ap*), earth (*pṛthivī*); it is the ether of Western occultism, the *ākāśa* of the Hindu doctrine.

We have no time now to dwell at length upon this body, but there are a few things we can say about it that can help us reflect. It is also called "vital" because, in actual fact, it gives life and cohesion to electronic and molecular elements (*bhūtas*). After all, it is of the physical order, and, although neither material nor solid, it feels a strong attraction toward the gross plane; a strong electro-magnetism connects it to the *bhūtas*, especially if it is *qualified* by what we might call earthly tendencies. This *prāṇa*-vital vehicle, made as image of the physical form, would last a very short time if cremation were carried out, as the solid, the liquid and the gaseous are solved by the power of the fire. In India this is practiced, while in ancient Egypt mummification was practiced, because by prolonging the life of the four elements (and thus of the visible physical body), the life of the *prāṇa* body, or the *ka* as it was called, lasted longer. But India has always favored that true or second death we have mentioned, while Egypt loved and was attached to the earth and the earthly. Through *prāṇa,* the visible gross physical body can be *perceived*, because, after all, we are within the physical dimension. Needless to say, a *yogi* abstracting himself from the visible physical (just so we can understand each other) is always capable of materializing himself in another visible body upon the dense physical plane.

The *manas* has the ability to mold the quintessence so as to produce effects at the level of the *bhūtas*.

Ākāśa is the mercury of the Philosophers, certainly not the elementary and natural mercury, and the initiated Alchemists knew this and sought to extract it from the most base and most corruptible mineral elements.

— What is the state of consciousness of the individual who finds himself in a pranic body?

R - It is a particular state of consciousness because, although he observes and perceives at a physical level, he has no access to it. It is like looking through a window where one can see and hear what is happening outside without being able to communicate. There are, however, some exceptions.

— Does this state offer possibilities to the advanced *yogi*?

R - We already said so. The true *yogi* avails of this state only for certain special reasons, because he considers the physical as the plane of non-reality, metallization and imprisonment.

— If one finds oneself within this *prāṇa* body, is it possible to carry out some rectifications of the mineral physical?

R - Yes. Here we are touching on a crucial point of the alchemical goal. It is only from this state of consciousness that one can act upon the mineral quaternary by means of *solve et coagula*. However, there may also be techniques for the extraction of the *volatile* from the *fixed* and for the fixation of the volatile. In conclusion, when one realizes the *quinta essentia,* with and by this, the various *bhūtas* can be manipulated. Remember that the *bhūtas* are already contained in the *ākāśa*, but only in the potential state; from this stems the possibility of acting upon the *bhūtas*.

— Another question on this topic: it is known that a number of great Masters willingly preserved their physical body for a long time; why?

R - Speaking in alchemical terms, we might say they did that in order to *fix* the spirit, which is volatile. The body, made *sattva*, acts as a *fixativum*, as a base, a support for the spirit, which on account of its particular nature, tends to expand and dilate. Well, let's go a step further and consider the solution of the *prāṇamaya* sheath. The entity, if the "firing" of the four remaining corporeal elements has not occurred, continues to abide in this body of expression for some time. However, not being a body unto itself, not being a definite and stable compound but simple vital energy, a bridge linking the *manas* and the strictly visible vehicle, it *disperses*. The physical body "decomposes" or "breaks down"; the *prāṇa*, being *air*, "disperses," so that it returns to the reservoir of the planetary *prāṇa* body. This process, too, occurs in a manner that the being barely notices; it causes neither pain nor anything else because it is a natural *process*. The entity deprived of the *prāṇa* body finds itself in another dimension, another state of consciousness, in a vibratory sphere other than the physical-*prāṇa* one. To the eyes of this entity, the physical world in its integrality disappeared; it no longer exists. At this point, all links with the gross world (*viśva*) are sundered; what happens in it is no longer either seen or perceived, contrary to what used to occur when it possessed a pranic body. And, paradoxically, one has not yet *left* the physical sphere.

— Having laid down the physical-*prāṇa* body, does the being find itself in the manasic one? And what is this *manas* mentioned so often?

R - The *manomaya* body is an amalgamation of thought and desire, of mind and sentiment, which we often speak of as *kāma-manas*. This vehicle of manifestation is the one that is hardest to die. This is the true body of illusion, of the psyche, of subconscious crystallization. In this psychic sphere many individuals drown, lose themselves, delay awareness of Self. It is the world of projections, the "astral" world of Western occultism. We can say that this world has no reality of its own because it is an accumulation of the image-forms created by the individualized *manas*.

If one seeks to perceive the archetypes or the universal ideas, one must ascend into the sphere of *buddhi* or *vijñānamaya*, that is, the sphere of principial consciousness.

— Is this the sphere of *taijasa* spoken of in *Vedānta* philosophy? Is it the intermediate zone between *viśva* and *prājña*?

R - Yes. The *manas* is the apex of individuality. Descending *buddhi* is the terminal aspect of universality. Beyond these subtle vehicles, there is *prājña,* or the first determination of being.

— When one leaves the physical body, does one come into contact with the *jīvātmā*?

R - Yes. However, it is possible to achieve this even when one is still in the physical body.

The disciple's *sādhanā* should lead to conscious realization of identity with the Self.

— In what terms can this encounter take place? And how does the *jīvātmā* present and express itself?

R - The *jīvātmā* can take the form preferred by the reflection of incarnate consciousness. In general, it reveals itself as a blazing but not blinding sun, or as a majestic, ethereal and luminous *Deva*.

Communication occurs by means of telepathy because the *jīvātmā* communicates, in fact, with its reflection.

— Is the *jīvātmā* an "alter ego" of the being?

R - In Western terms, we might say that the *jīvātmā* represents the Soul, while the *ātma* or *ātman* is the Spirit, which, in turn, is of the nature of *Brahman*.

— Therefore, if it is not a being outside of ourselves, why do we not recognize this "Clear Light" of which the *Bardo Thötröl* speaks?

R - The reflection of consciousness found in the physical and subtle incarnation—having the same powers, though reduced, as the *jīvātmā*—has built its own world, its own projections and its own appearances, to the point of becoming alienated and partly divided from its source.

Today we experience this state of consciousness, and when we encounter *ourselves* at other levels, we no longer recognize ourselves. We have lost our soul's identity, like a madman who at *manas* level no longer recognizes his individual identity.[1]

— Is this why we are called fallen Angels or sleeping Gods?

R - Yes. By "falling" into the individualized and into alienation we have lost sight of the source from which we are born. However, this kind of "fall" is not absolute but is apparent, because the incarnate reflection of consciousness is simply shrouded, veiled or has fallen asleep.

— So, however wakeful we are, we are asleep?

R - Yes. You said just now that we are sleeping Gods. From this stems the incitement to *Awaken*. The Awakened is one who has resolved this torpor, which *Vedānta* calls *avidyā* or *māyā*.

— Does one see the *jīvātmā* immediately after having left the physical body or after having gone through a number of other experiences upon the subtle plane?

R - I don't think that there are any fixed rules. The mode and moment of encounter are of the individual or karmic order, as "death" itself and re-birth are experiences of a personal order, whereby there cannot be events and

---

[1] See the chapter "The *Jīva* within the Form," in Raphael, *Beyond the Illusion of the Ego, op. cit.*

behaviors that are the same for everybody. We are not giving a vision of principle.

— So, therefore, it can occur before or after what is defined as the recapitulation of incarnate life?

R - Yes. I think so. There are no absolute norms in such things.

Q - There is mention of the recapitulation of life experiences, but what in actual fact does this represent?

R - It represents subconscious crystallization projected upon the screen of our own *aura*. This experience, too, may sometimes be achieved during physical incarnation.

— I wish to know if the Realized have these experiences just the same.

R - A Liberated has burnt out all subconscious residue, becoming spotless Light. The Liberated has no past, no history and therefore no future. The Liberated no longer lives upon projections or veiling superimpositions.

— (the first questioner) Now, in order to dissolve these subconscious remains—emotions, feelings, ideals, etc.—must one find oneself on the subtle plane, or can they be transcended while one remains on the physical plane? Can the *kāma* and *manas* bodies be transcended even at the physical incarnation level? I mean to say: must the second death (*manas* and *kāma*), of which Saint Paul speaks, occur on the subtle planes, or can it happen on the physical plane?

R - The manasic, pranic and physical are not three distinct and opposite levels. When in incarnation the individual possesses all three of them, he need not await entry into the subtle (*taijasa*).

The true death of the philosophers is actualized upon the gross physical level. To try to postpone the problem of "death" is an alibi on the part of the ego to perpetuate itself.

— How long can the *jīvātmā*'s vehicles or bodies prolong their existence?

R - We know that for Buddhism there are five *skandhas*. These, more than bodies in the sense we usually attribute to the word, are five psychological aspects or energetic aggregates that comprise individuality (*rūpa,* material form; *vedanā,* sensation; *saṁjñā,* perception; *saṁskāra,* concept; *vijñāna,* coordinating consciousness).

As long as there are particular qualities to be externalized, these must express and manifest themselves.

— Therefore, can I free myself of these *skandhas* only when I have transcended every possible kind of attraction-repulsion quality?

R - There is no doubt that as long as desire operates in us, we shall always go where it leads us. Where our passion is, there will our heart be.

— Reading some texts that refer to our topic, I have noticed that there are a number of contradictions. For example, some state that *karma* alone determines action upon the subtle plane, so the entity is really a passive object of its own *karma*. Somebody else says that the entity is free to determine itself; in fact, as it must become incarnate, it may choose the *matrix* of its birth.

Why this contradiction?

R - I don't think there are any contradictions. The determination of the entity subsists insofar as it has succeeded in dominating its "powers." But this occurs at a physical level too

— I agree that one must be prepared for certain events. Without doubt it is not sufficient for me to know that I myself can be that "Clear White Light"; I must be ready to realize it.

R - Look, thousands of people know of the existence of the soul, of the *ātman* and so on, but very few know how to realize themselves as *ātman*. On the other hand, one must distinguish between intellectual knowledge and realization.

Q - In other words, one must be?

R - We have often said so. If realization consisted only of memorizing all the *Vedānta*, Buddhist, texts, etc., everything would be so easy. But, unfortunately, things are different. It is not sufficient to read the *Bardo Thötröl*; one must be prepared to face the *events* of the *Bardo*. If we are not the "central point" on the physical plane (*viśva*), we shall never be it on the subtle (*taijasa*) plane. If we fail to face events upon the physical plane by applying appropriate detachment, we shall not be able to achieve success upon the subtle plane either.

Some think that once they have cast off their physical "clothing," they will become wiser. This is a gross error of judgment.

The majority part of human beings, having cast off their physical "clothing," find themselves within the intermediate subtle sphere, which is illusory.

For *Asparśa*, even the *prājña* (causal) state represents the root of *avidyā*, and *prājña* (*Dharmakāya* for the *Bardo Thötröl*) is beyond the physical and psychic; it is the state in which *savikalpa samādhi* is experienced, the highest *samādhi* upon the manifest plane.[1]

Q - From what I have heard, must I deduce that, paradoxically for my crystallizations, death doesn't exist?

R - Death, in the common sense, does not really exist. What we call death is governed by the *Śiva*-Principle, which means that death is simply a trans-formation, that is, a going beyond form (*rūpa*). It is a simple change of the state of consciousness, which, I repeat, for some may occur in such an unconscious manner as not to be perceived.

---

[1] For a realizative succession of these states, see Śaṅkara, *Aparokṣānubhūti: Self-Realization* (forthcoming from Aurea Vidyā, New York); and for the various types of *samādhi*, see *Dṛgdṛśyaviveka: Discernment between ātman and non-ātman*, Translation from the Sanskrit and Commentary by Raphael (New York: Aurea Vidyā, 2008).

Most humans, especially in the West, have been unable and continue to be unable to establish a proper relationship with death. Dramatization of the event, attachment to form, identification with earthly ideals, etc., prove to be disappointing and infantile to those who know.

Sooner or later it will become clear that birth falls under the law of *limitation*, while death is under that of liberation.[1]

Q - So should life be an intelligent training for death?

R - If possible, for triple death. Many are so engrossed in *doing* that the physical plane seems to be the only one in existence. Often one of life's levels is rendered absolute, although, despite its apparent validity, it is neither absolute nor determining.

Some people are so attached to their desires, to their ideals, to their family, political or social ideals, etc., that they consider their existence upon the physical plane eternal.

There is a tendency to overdramatize life and death; there is too much exaltation, sometimes theatricality, in human behavior.

On the world's stage there is such a degree of identification with oneself that one tends to forget that one's true *role* involves simple apparition and disappearance. Some even pay a high price for their *interpretation*, especially after death.

---

[1] See the chapter "Bodily Death," in Raphael, *Tat tvam asi, op. cit.*

Q - Forgive me if I return to my problem, but I would like, if it is possible, an accessible interpretation of the *Bardo*.

What do the so-called "wrathful and peaceful deities" of the second *Bardo* mean?

What can *Ratnasaṁbhava*, *Amitābha*, *Amoghasiddhi*, etc., mean to us Westerners?

R - A teaching is designed for a particular people; it has its own language, and it gives a particular name and form to certain qualities that are universal principles or individual energetic qualities. Jesus Christ, too, is the personification of a universal principle.

Certainly it is difficult for the Christian to recognize *Amitābha* or *Amoghasiddhi*. However, if we depart from this premise, we can better understand what the individual sees in the second *Bardo*.

At this point, it is necessary to go more thoroughly into the dynamics of psychic processes, into how they come about, how they crystallize and how they manifest themselves on the *taijasa* plane.

According to Buddhism, to which the *Bardo Thötröl* belongs, the three bodies or states of Being are:

— *Dharmakāya*

— *Saṁbhogakāya*

— *Nirmāṇakāya*

Through the first *Bardo*, to which we referred a while back, one realizes *Dharmakāya*, the body of primordial Illumination. This takes us out of *saṁsāra*-becoming because identity with the "Clear White Light" is achieved.

If *Dharmakāya* is not realized, one enters into the state of consciousness of *Saṁbhogakāya*, or *Hiraṇyagarbha* for *Vedanta*, the subtle condition with all its subdivisions. It is within this sphere that the individual's karmic projections gradually take form.

We said earlier that failure to recognize the *jīvātmā* occurs because the reflection of the incarnate consciousness identifies with its subconscious contents, with its projections. We might say that the gravitational power of the subconscious content holds the consciousness down upon the individualized plane.

Now, once we have lost the opportunity of integrating with the "Clear Light," a kind of drama involving the incarnate consciousness and its projections or "shadows" takes place.

How is subconscious content born? Our psychic spatiality is a part of the universal "substance" or *prakṛti*, or the χώρα according to Plato; our minds are a part of the universal mind. When we think at length about an event or repeatedly express a quality—for example, love, hate, envy, greed, etc.—our psychic "substance" or our *śakti* molds itself to the point of condensation, becoming *mass*; that is, energy solidifies, taking with it the qualification externalized by the consciousness.[1] A reiterated idea becomes a *qualified entity,* capable of provoking harmony or disharmony. The individual is a creator, but he forgets this; therefore he weaves the web of happiness or sorrow according to the *constructions* erected within his own psychic spatiality. Thus, a crystallized content is a psychic

---

[1] For an in-depth review of the theme, see the chapter "The Origin of Subconsciousness," in Raphael, *Tat tvam asi, op. cit.*

entity that remains within our vital circumference until it is resolved or dissolved.

— If, for example, I express hate, what happens in my psychic circumference?

R - Little by little your "substance" molds itself and becomes sensitive to the point of crystallizing or solidifying the quality.

— Then, if this crystallization is transferred onto the subtle *Saṁbhogakāya* plane, what happens?

R - The projection of the "wrathful deities," of which we spoke before, occurs. If we consider that the subtle or *Saṁbhogakāya* plane is formal, we must agree that every idea or psychic content at this level will appear as a *form*, a symbol, a body-instrument. Upon the plane of the manifest, Life expresses itself by means of qualities, availing of a material support or formal instrument (*rūpa*). Thus, in this case, the quality of hatred in the subtle plane manifests itself through a *form*, which may even take the likeness of an animal or a demon, with specific features, which tries to attack us. This condition occurs in dreams when a strange "form" (animal, demon, etc.) assails us. Terrified, we try to escape but are held down. Our psychic monsters are the other side of ourselves. We store up our violence, and, at the opportune moment, it turns against us. We are condemned or raised up by the quality of our crystallized thoughts. In dreams, anguish is banished by awakening, but within the subtle state, there is no way out for anguish, and we must undergo it to the end. In other words, we are devoured by our own projections, conceptions and qualifications.

— So the devil exists then?

R - The devil (*heruka*) is the "personification" of our disharmony, of our mistaken use of energy, of our crystallized violence. The devil is the negative side of the individual and can take on a particular shape; it is the figment of the ego's opposition, of its wickedness, etc. In the Western initiatory Tradition, there is mention of "descent into the underworld," which represents a stage toward the achievement of liberation.[1]

Q - Therefore, are these projections of the "wrathful deities," or of the *herukas,* nothing but our crystallizations? Can we not neutralize these powers when we reach the subtle plane?

R - When we reach it, it will be too late, because there we shall be lived and dragged down by our samsaric phantoms.

It happens, we repeat, as in a dream: we are lived by our dreams, we are made powerless by them. During incarnation, we accumulate contents that we project in due time. It is as if we were winding a clock, which at the opportune moment inevitably unwinds.

---

[1] For the "descent into the underworld," see the chapter "Orphic Ascesis," in Raphael, *Orphism and the Initiatory Tradition, op. cit.*

— Unfortunately, one forgets that an emotion or an idea takes form.

R - Yes, that's true. When the individual becomes aware of being a *molder* of things, of events and forms, he will pay greater attention to understanding the law of right "construction."

— I presume that the projection of the "peaceful deities" must proceed in the same way as that of the "wrathful deities."

R - Naturally. The individual experiences his *qualities*, let's call them good or bad, in a concrete manner, and each quality-content expresses itself through particular forms (*rūpas*). Paradise and hell are the products of our ideations. "We become what we think," says the *Upaniṣad*.

Q - How can we exit from these qualified forms, which bring us into anguish or into pleasure?

R - Yes, you said the right thing, "into pleasure" as well. This is very important if you want to exit from the sphere of *Saṁbhogakāya* and enter into that of *Dharmakāya*, that is, the plane of formless and primordial pure Light, where dualism vanishes. It is inevitable that the task of transformation must be undertaken upon the gross physical plane. The *Bardo Thötröl*, we repeat, is not a teaching for the dead, but for the living, also because there is no death. We must dissolve crystallized dualism, we must "unburden" our subconsciousness when we are in the physical body, so that we make ourselves free to realize the state of *Dharmakāya*, or, if ready, the state of *Svabhāvikakāya*, which is equivalent to *Vedānta's Fourth* or *Turīya*. To think of transcending the dualism of *Saṁbhogakāya* without realizing oneself here and now means falling into a gross error of judgment, which, at the given moment, will prove extremely costly.

Q - (the former questioner) If the solution fails to occur, must one try the third *Bardo*, that is, the *Sidpa Bardo*?

R - Whoever fails to realize the Self must necessarily return to the pathway of individualization.

— Leaving aside all theological conceptualizations, what is the psychological and practical reason for reincarnation?

R - We consider the term transmigration better suited to the state of the experimenting ego.[1] First of all, we must consider that it is an effect and not a cause. The cause of transmigration into the different individualized states is represented by unresolved *vāsanās* and *saṁskāras*, which perpetuate themselves within our vital spatiality.

What happens when we find ourselves in *Saṁbhogakāya* without having dissolved our contents?

---

[1] See also the chapter "Transmigration," in Raphael, *The Pathway of Non-duality, op. cit.*, and the chapter "Transmigration," in Raphael, *Tat tvam asi, op. cit.*

The seeds, which are by now at the potential state, gradually try to sprout and blossom, and so the entity is led to where they may be expressed.

Transmigration occurs, therefore, because some unburned seeds seek manifestation. There is nothing mysterious in this process; we might say it is simple, "scientific" and consequential.

As long as the *thirst* for something persists, experimentation and incarnation persist too. The third *Bardo* is the inevitable effect of the non solution of the *saṁskāras* and of the *ahaṁkāra*, the "sense of ego."

AHAṀKĀRA

Questioner - Excuse me if I pose this question in a certain manner, but if we wish to understand some things, we must free ourselves of those sentimental conceptions that often hide or fail to reveal the truth. You have spoken of "sense of ego," of *ahaṁkāra*, sometimes of "I am this" and expressions like this. Seeking to eliminate from truth the sentimental emotional superimpositions of which Śaṅkara himself also speaks, I ask: in what does this "sense of ego" consist, what lies behind the term *ahaṁkāra*?

Raphael - It is axiomatic that the universe is governed by laws and not by feelings, even if these, in particular circumstances and at the individual level, can trigger the application or operation of a law. We have spoken of *post mortem* as an event regulated by specific laws, and a law can be surpassed by applying another law. It is important to understand which *means* favor the application of a law. We normally consider the ultimate end, not the means, and this is a grave error. Liberation, for example, is the ultimate aim of the individual, and many are obsessed by the end rather than by the beginning.

The *ahaṁkāra* is a "prism" that decomposes the *buddhi*'s central fire-light.[1]

— Therefore, is the *ahaṁkāra* a mirror that reflects within us the color-qualities of our nature?

R   Yes. The qualities or the various "colorations" of the *prakṛti* substance.

— Now, why, with reference to *ahaṁkāra,* do you say "I am this"?

R - The prism is also life, therefore also consciousness; in nature there is nothing devoid of life and consciousness, that is, of being (*sat*) and of awareness (*cit*).

Thus this prism refracts certain color-qualities of the *buddhi*, often deforming them, and the reflection of consciousness objectified by the prism identifies with or adheres to the single colorations.

— Why does it deform the qualities or colors? Is there a valid, rational reason?

R - Deformation occurs thanks to the *manas*, which is the psychic instrument that tries to grasp and describe the objective reality of forms. *Manas* creates truths that are not such, so that, depending on memory (the subconscious), it superimposes upon pure reality things that do not belong to it.

---

[1] See Raphael, *The Threefold Pathway of Fire*, especially the chapter "The Empirical Ego," *op. cit.*

— Therefore does *ahaṁkāra*, identifying itself with a particular color of the central Fire, believe itself to be that color?

R - Yes. A process of assimilation occurs, producing "I am this." And the assimilation, the identification, is such that it disowns all other colors.

— But can this "filter" not reflect the entire luminous compound of the central Fire, or is it destined to reflect only certain colors?

R - It is inevitable that *ahaṁkāra* particularizes, selects and breaks down the central universal Fire. It represents the *principium individuationis*, the principle of individualization of the universal quality-consciousness.

— So, does unity become multiplicity for it, and the homogeneous heterogeneous?

R - Yes. The unity of the *buddhi* permeated with *sattva*, through *ahaṁkāra*, becomes multiplicity and heterogeneity in *manas*; furthermore, every experience is referred to a *me*.

— In brief, is the white light refracted into its individual units of color?

R - Certainly. Through this "psychic prism," we consider ourselves white, green, red, yellow, etc., and each of us defends his own identity and his own existential condition.

— This leads me to the conclusion that as long as *ahaṁkāra* exists the individual remains an individual in opposition to other color-individuals.

R - This is an inevitable consequence.

— Now, if we speak, with reference to the human being, of realization and of manifestation of the universal principle, does this mean that this "psychic prism" can be avoided or transcended?

R - Yes, indeed. Otherwise the individual could never be complete and unity.

— In what way, then, can this limiting mirror be shattered?

R - At this point, the various types of *yoga* intervene, which, in their proper perspective, have a sole aim: that of dissolving the limiting "prism" or "sense of ego" as a factor in individualization and differentiation.

— Is this how we find ourselves centered in the *buddhi*?

R - Yes. The *buddhi* is "substance" that contains the three *guṇas* or the three fundamental, essential qualities of life. Or we might also say that the *buddhi* contains the "essences" of the universal *qualities*. The combinations of the three *guṇa*-qualities are countless, so we may express multiple combinations of qualities.

— What relation is there between *buddhi* and *jīvātmā*?

R - The *buddhi* is the negative pole, the *jīvātmā* the positive pole, and from their union and interrelationship, the "psychic prism," or *ahaṁkāra,* is born. This, and therefore also the *manas,* is the outcome of a polar combination.

— Through the *buddhi,* the *jīvātmā* considers itself as universal existential center; while through the *manas*, with the "prism" conditioning, it sees itself as individual center.
Is that the way things stand?

R - Yes. The empirical "I" resembles the reflection of sun upon water.

— You said before that the aim of *yoga* is to resolve the individualizing factor. However, as far as I know, some branches of psychology try to achieve this individualization process. How can this be explained?

R - There are consciousnesses that have turned themselves into "mass" and have dispersed themselves, not into the *buddhi,* which is unity of universal synthesis, but into the collective subconscious, into the collective formless, amorphous chaos. It is inevitable that for these people a process of synthesis and unity is necessary; first of all, at the level of human individuality, they must emerge from a state of group consciousness and recognize themselves as individuals. But whoever is already an individual with his own particular center of integrated consciousness must achieve another synthesis, which is the universal synthesis.

— Does this mean the consciousness molds itself upon the universal archetype?

R - Yes.

— Eugène Canseliet, in his Introduction to Fulcanelli's *The Dwellings of the Philosophers,* writes: "Here, from an alchemical point of view, resides the indispensable awakening of consciousness, within this harmonic phenomenon, which springs from the control of two extraneous rhythms and, thanks to which, the human soul can attune its own rhythm with the universe's diapason and free itself from the limited sphere of the individual."[1] Can we say that this corresponds to what we are dealing with?

R - Yes. Being is a vital Point capable of solving its own existential problems insofar as it attunes itself to the universal. But this means having to abandon its particular expressive center. We have already spoken about this.[2]

— Does the danger of "abandonment," of letting go of feelings and instincts, etc., consist in the possibility of falling into the subconscious state?

R - Yes. Premature abandonment may lead not into *buddhi,* and therefore to supraconsciousness, but into the

---

[1] Fulcanelli, *Le Dimore Filosofali* [*The Dwellings of the Philosophers*] (Rome: Edizioni Mediterranee [Italian edition], 1973).

[2] Refer to the chapter "Vibrating Life" in this same book.

individual and often even into the collective subconscious. The danger of drugs, for example, lies in this.

— Does "consciousness of ego," therefore, have a validity of its own upon the empirical plane?

R - Everything is in its right place. As we said, *ahaṁkāra* individualizes, and this act of individualization may offer precise though limited existential experiences.

— Does the *jīvātmā*, through the eye of the *buddhi* characterized by *sattva*, see the entire range of colors?

R - Yes. Without the "prism" that divides and particularizes, the *jīvātmā* is capable of seeing reality in its *totality*, synthesis and unity. This implies that its relationship with things changes, that its vision extends and becomes inclusive, becoming harmony within Harmony.

SEPARATION

Questioner - When discussing the *post mortem*, we spoke about the separation of the *prāṇa* body from the gross physical dimension. Can the detachment that is undergone passively be realized in an active and conscious way?

Raphael - To realize this, one must avoid breaking the threads of life and of consciousness, which are anchored in the heart and in the head; otherwise one enters another state of being, that of *manas*. It is inevitable that "separation" of the *prāṇa*-body from the gross one without altering the "threads" of union is a "Herculean feat." It is more difficult to extract gold than to make it.

— (same questioner) However, once the volatile has been separated from the fixed, is the individual free to act upon matter?

R - Yes. From this existential state and with solar Dignity, one may act upon *ākāśa*, upon the material quintessence, which contains within it the four bodily elements and is susceptible to endless manipulation. We have already spoken about this.

— Does this imply defeating death?

R - Let us say that it does. That which the layman experiences in an unconscious and inescapable manner at the moment of passing or disintegration of the physical body, the Initiated alchemist, and the *yogi* too, experiences in a conscious and deliberate way. The layman is under the law of necessity, the Initiated under the law of freedom; for the Initiated, there is neither death nor necessity.

— In the Eleusinian and the Egyptian Mysteries, was a conscious effort made to master the process of death or "withdrawal"?

R - Yes, but this was not the only motive. The Occident also had and still has a metaphysics that goes beyond the gross and subtle manifest dimensions.

Anyway, don't speak as if "separation" were so easy. Those who have attempted it know that. One must overcome certain "forces" that, despite the ability of the operator, tenaciously oppose the free flow of ascent and descent. Furthermore, there are real dangers that often make the undertaking inadvisable. Playing with Fire one may *literally* get burnt.

— I have heard that sometimes the body of a deceased Initiated has not being found in the tomb. Is this true?

R - Yes, very true.

— What law did the adept apply in order to make the body vanish?

R - That of Einstein, the law that has always existed from the beginning of the world. In other words, they transformed mass into energy.

— What causes those transformations that occur during withdrawal of the physically solid into the pranic and manasic?

R - Science tells us that all metallic and chemical products compose and decompose. The molecules aggregate and desegregate, so that matter is constantly in transmutation; but what *agent* causes this "unbinding" and "binding," this *solve et coagula*? According to Alchemy, it is Fire. Now, within our *athanor* we should be able to find this Fire, which, once ignited, sets the transformation process in motion. It is obvious that this is no vulgar fire, but the Fire of the Philosophers, that invisible yet active, enveloping, penetrating and resolving Fire.[1]

In *Filum Ariannae*, 75, we read: "Without Fire matter is useless and the Philosopher's Mercury is a chimera that lives only in our imagination. It is from the regime of the Fire that everything depends."

Q - I can guess the kind of Fire you mean; therefore I wish to know how that Fire can be ignited?

---

[1] See Raphael, *The Threefold Pathway of Fire*, in particular the chapter "Fire of Life: Realization according to Alchemy," *op. cit.*

R - There are various *means* and each of the various schools of initiation can utilize the one handed down to it by its own tradition. I wish to point out, however, that to light the Fire, measure out its "regime," raise it up to the Heavens, realize the *androgyne* and conquer back immortality can be compared to a "Herculean labor," and very few have the *patience* and the qualifications to actualize it.

— What is the value of the mastery of one plane of life toward the attainment of metaphysical Realization?

R - It must be said that dominating an existential plane and knowing how to enter and exit it, although constituting a great conquest and offering many operative possibilities, does not mean having yet realized the fullness of the resplendent and incommensurable *ātman*. Were a person to conquer the entire world and become its supreme lord while failing to conquer back himself as *ātman-Brahman*, he would simply remain within the world of *māyā* and duality.

Q - But is Alchemy not a complete traditional teaching?

R - If we transpose the alchemical symbols into the principial dimension, then *materia prima,* or quintessence of the gross state, is represented in *Sāṁkhya* by universal *Prakṛti,* or by primordial Waters; and sulfur, the sun or king, is represented by *Puruṣa,* or by supreme Spirit.

From this perspective, the alchemical symbols are interpreted according to the degree of the researcher's consciousness. Some even interpret them in chemical, metallic and material terms; they seek common, commercial and utilitarian gold.

It is necessary, therefore, to distinguish between chemical, spagyric alchemy, which is a mere degeneration of Alchemy, and alchemy interested in the initiatory Lesser Mysteries, and Alchemy that focuses upon the Greater Mysteries. We can have the Lesser *Opus* or the Greater *Opus*.

ĀKĀŚA AND MEDITATION

Questioner - This evening, if my friends agree, I again would like to take up the question of meditation, but from certain perspectives.

There are many erroneous and misleading concepts about meditation. Furthermore, it is considered differently depending on the school of thought followed. I, however, believe that meditation is a means that triggers certain laws. Recently you spoke about *means* that need to be utilized to achieve certain ends. First of all, is meditation a means?

Raphael - Yes, indeed, and a very potent one too.

— (same questioner) Now, is there a mystical and a *yoga* meditation? A passive and a creative meditation?

R - Let's say yes, the former uses sentiment as support, the latter *manas* or mind.

— In his *Yogasūtras*,[1] Patañjali says that meditation means fixing the mind for a long time upon a content or

---

[1] Patañjali, *The Regal Way to Realization (Yogadarśana)*, Translation from the Sanskrit and Commentary by Raphael (New York: Aurea Vidyā, 2012).

object of meditation. I wish to go back to Alchemy and consider meditation as an instrument of *solve et coagula.* This implies that meditation, properly used, can dissolve something or eventually coagulate an archetype. However, if the right position of consciousness is not found, we don't have dissolution or coagulation. Is this correct?

R - Yes, certainly. Please continue.

— Now the point is this: how many elements are required to effect a perfect meditation?

R - A correct consciential position, a plastic and responsive "substance" as matrix of creation, appropriate fire capable of bringing a *pratyaya* (mental content, object of concentration) to correct firing, and lastly, content, object to be molded (*pratyaya*).

— In this subject, I believe that the position of consciousness is of enormous importance. Could you give us a detailed account of this point?

R - Last time we spoke about *ahaṁkāra.* Well, this "sense of ego" through the *manas* has *molded* numerous events, phantoms, image-forms and crystallized, coagulated deformations, to such an extent as to enslave the consciousness completely. Our task today is that of resolving that huge chaotic mass of crystallizations and freeing that imprisoned reflection of consciousness.

Meditation represents a valid instrument of *solution* of the crystallized underworld and of *fixing* consciousness in *buddhi.* It is clear that in order to dissolve these crystallizations, maculations, lower or subconscious figments, it is extremely important to comprehend upon which level one must operate to carry out the *solve et coagula* process.

We mentioned previously that the gross physical plane is formed of five symbolic elements represented by earth, water, air, fire and ether. *Ākāśa* is the quintessence of matter (whose corresponding superior element is universal *ākāśa* or primordial Waters), and all the other elements (fire, air, etc., or solid, liquid and gas, etc.) spring from it. We are composed of metals, minerals and chemical elements, which all owe their origin to *ākāśa*. If we keep this in mind, we can easily understand that to re-mold a *body* one must operate or meditate upon the *ākāśa* level through the solar fire of *manas*. However, this kind of meditation belongs to *Haṭhayoga*, which aims at bestowing long life, harmony and health upon the body. On the contrary, the task of those who wish to *resolve* the *ahaṃkāra* is another, whereby the position of consciousness shifts and the *materia prima* upon which to operate changes.

In the former case, we avail of *manas* as the molding fire and *ākāśa* as the material to be molded; in the latter case, we have *manas* as the material to be molded and the sattvic *buddhi* as our molding fire. This implies that one needs to "separate" fire and air from earth and water, then with the power of Fire to dissolve individualized air of the *manas*, recomposing or coagulating it on the new archetype. In order to act as support to all this, the state of consciousness must find itself at the deepest level of being; otherwise, the creative meditative operation will be ineffective.[1]

---

[1] See the chapter "Meditation," in Raphael, *The Threefold Pathway of Fire, op. cit.*

— So, in order to transform oneself, it is not sufficient
to sit cross-legged and pray with one's lips. This I think
is quite clear, isn't it?

R - "This people honors me with their lips, but its
heart is far from me," says Jesus. More often than not,
meditation represents simple reflection upon mental content, a mechanical repetition of sounds or words or some
imagination of symbols.

Sometimes an improvement of one's psycho-physical
state is obtained, and this is already something for many.

— So, is the position of consciousness of those who seek
to transform the *manas* to be found behind the *manas* itself?

R - Yes, naturally. As the *manas* is behind the five elements, therefore behind the material *ākāśa*, so the *buddhi*
is behind *manas*. As long as one operates within the
ambit of the individualized, it is sufficient to use *manas*
as one's operative instrument; but if one wishes to break
one's individualized circumference, one must enter *buddhi*.

All this may also be related to the *Qabbālāh*. So, if
one wishes to operate upon *Yesod* and *Malkuth* one must
choose the *sephirah Hod* as one's molding fire. *Hod* is
the sphere of magic, but also of the individualized psyche.
If one wishes to act upon *Hod*, one's consciousness must
abandon the lower quaternary and enter *Tiphereth*, which
represents the supraindividual sphere.[1]

---

[1] For this Teaching, see Raphael, *The Pathway of Fire according
to the Qabbālāh*, *op. cit.*

DYING TO ONESELF

Questioner - This evening I wish to ask what kind of good this earthly plane can offer so that thousands of individuals feel attracted to it to the point of paroxysm?

Raphael - You were absent when we discussed this question. So, I'd like to refer the question to someone else. What do you think the earthly mode of life has to offer?

— (same questioner) Qualities typical of the human individuality, without doubt.

— (another speaker) I have come to the conclusion that human experience is characterized by an ambition to have and possess. To have intelligence, a family, money, social status, power over others, etc.

R - May we accept this conclusion?

— (another speaker) I don't know whether it is the same thing, but I would say that the human experience is characterized by the manifestation of *manas* and *kāma* qualities.

R - Qualities inherent to the ego, used to swell and gratify the psychological ego?

— Yes, to realize the ego.

— (first speaker) And if someone living in such an oppressive world, at least for me, no longer has any *ambition* to "have" or to do, where should he go?

R - In the universe there are many, many modes and expressions of life, and one must simply wait until one's psycho-physical form liberates one's consciousness and directs it toward conditions more in keeping with one's vibratory state.

— Can there be moral factors that prevent us from abandoning something or from turning our backs upon those experiences that have no further meaning for us?

R - It is not a question of morals, but of *vibrations*. If for you this mode of life has no further meaning, then all you must do, as you put it, is turn your back on it and joyfully await the liberation of consciousness from the prison of form or σῶμα-σῆμα as Plato states.[1]

— I asked this question because, at least I hope so, the only thing I must free myself from is morality, a guilt complex. I don't know if I explained my idea properly.

R - Yes, certainly. As long as we are bound by contents, be they positive or negative, we are held within imprisoning circumferences. If you simply wish to *escape*,

---

[1]   For the terms *sôma* (body-form) and *sêma* (tomb-prison), see Raphael, *Initiation into the Philosophy of Plato, op. cit.*

then this would be a wrong movement. But if your consciousness is a "fully ripened fruit," let go, don't create any resistance, abandon yourself to the power of reintegration. When the fire has achieved its goal, it is free to quench itself, and *nirvāṇa* will reveal itself in all its majestic beatitude, devoid of having and possessing.

Q - If I use this attitude of conscious detachment, of simple witness of the comings and goings of life, of spectator looking down, as it were, at the chaotic movement of men from the peak of a mountain, would I be in the proper position? Or is there a more efficacious way of implementing my yearning to return to *That*?

Consider the fact that I avail myself of no techniques, attend no spiritual meetings and seek no *guru*, as all this seems to be but a pretext of the ego.

If one fails to die to what one is, it is unlikely one may succeed elsewhere. You see, I don't believe that there is anything to be *reached*. I don't try to transcend myself, I make no effort to impose discipline upon myself, I simply attempt "dying" to all. Every now and then I feel some slight inclination toward desire, the ambition to act, and so I ask myself who is it inside me that desires and wants. When I ask myself this question, it seems to me that the externalized motion ceases and peace returns. I experience my modest *karma* with detachment, as if it belonged to another, thinking that what is born must die, while the *me* within me is eternal, immortal. I am deeply convinced of, I might even say I have faith in, my infiniteness, so that I accept my temporal limitations serenely.

I have given you an account of my position of consciousness because it is the first time that, relating to

someone who has already travelled along the pathway, I
am in a position to confirm the validity or otherwise of
my attitude. I'm sorry if I dwelt at length on the subject.

R - I thank you from the heart for the precious gift
you have offered us. There is nothing more beautiful than
contemplating the vital movement of *māyā* from the Witness's point of view. In the presence of *comprehension*
and *maturity,* which spur one toward reintegration, there is
nothing more appropriate than being in the world without
being of the world.

I don't know if you have ever observed schools of
children busy playing: what joy to watch their movements,
their tears, their laughter, their doubts, their falls, to hear
their cries, to perceive their exchanges of energy, to see
how clumsy they are, how absorbed they are in what
they are doing. In the presence of beauty, one need not
make a move, a gesture or ask oneself any questions. All
problems vanish: there is pure contemplation. Only the
detached Witness is capable of perceiving the beauty of
the multiform expression of life. Whoever finds himself on
the mountain top of "divine indifference" can contemplate
the movement of millions of children who cry, exult, fall
and pick themselves up again, clash, meet, open and close
themselves like a flower at sundown. A Witness moves
within the human interstices without being attracted or
repulsed by the electromagnetic power of the entities. A
Witness has ceased to be in order to Be, has ceased to
live in order to Live, has ceased to do and act because
he lives on his axis of rotational movement.

As our brother quite properly stated, there is nothing to be reached, no effort required; there is only one thing to be done: to die daily to oneself.

O sweet and ineffable "death of the Philosophers," what a gift you have to offer to those who have comprehended you, to those who have rent your veil and looked upon your bare nudity and illusion!

INDEX

Absolute 7, 21, 25, 26, 29, 30, 31, 38, 39, 40, 41, 44, 49, 53, 55, 58, 64, 70, 85, 87, 104, 110, 120, 127, 128, 142, 143, 147.

Advaita 11, 30, 64, 65, 66, 67, 83.

ahaṁkāra 154, 155, 156, 157, 158, 159, 161, 170, 171.

ākāśa 117, 119, 136, 137, 138, 163, 169, 171, 172.

Alchemy 48, 165, 166, 167, 170

Amitābha 148.

Amoghasiddhi 148.

ānanda 45, 78.

Asparśa 48, 64, 65, 124, 129.

    Asaparśayoga 30, 121.

    Asaparśvāda 13, 38, 48, 49, 64, 83, 87, 122, 132, 133.

āśrama 100.

ātman 21, 53, 59, 68, 69, 72, 92, 133, 141, 145, 166.

avidyā 73, 74, 93, 123, 142, 146.

Bardo 133, 134, 141, 145, 146, 148, 152, 153, 154.

    Bardo Thötröl 133, 134, 141, 145, 146, 148, 152.

    Sidpa Bardo 153.

Beatitude 12, 18, 37, 45, 66, 93, 95, 96, 121, 128, 175.

Bhagavadgītā 34.

Gītā 123.

bhakti 125.

bhūta 68, 136, 137, 138.

Brahman 14, 27, 28, 31, 65, 69, 72, 84, 86, 91, 113, 124, 141, 166.

    nirguṇa Brahman 113.

    saguṇa Brahman 113.

Buddha 15, 120.

buddhi 87, 103, 140, 157, 158, 159, 161, 171, 172.

Buddhism 48, 79, 144, 148.

Christianity 79.

Clear White Light 145, 148.

Completeness 12, 35, 36, 37, 67, 98, 130.

Consciousness 11, 13, 14, 15, 17, 20, 35, 39, 41, 52, 53, 56, 57, 61, 67, 68, 75, 81, 82, 83, 87, 92, 95, 100, 105, 114, 118, 119, 121, 122, 125, 130, 131, 133, 134, 135, 137, 138, 139, 140, 141, 142, 144, 146, 149, 152, 156, 157, 159, 160, 161, 163, 166, 170, 171, 172, 174, 175.

Constant 12, 29, 31, 36, 37, 38, 40, 53, 56, 57, 120, 165.

darśana 63, 64, 67.

Death of the philosophers 144, 177.

Demiurge 15, 118, 119.

deva 68, 69, 141.

dharma 34, 56, 80, 122, 134, 146, 148, 149, 152, 153.

Dharmakāya 146, 148, 149, 152, 153.

Egypt 48, 137.

Egyptian Mysteries 164. See also Mysteries.

Ethics 98.

Fall of the soul 75. See also Soul.

Fourth 44, 53, 153.

Gauḍapāda 64, 68.

God 11, 19, 28, 29, 46, 60, 75, 76, 77, 78, 79, 112, 125, 142.

Greater Mysteries 167. See also Mysteries.

Greater *Opus* 167. See also *Opus*.

guṇa 68, 95, 113, 125, 158.

guru 86, 88, 91, 175.

Harmony 12, 14, 16, 17, 47, 78, 94, 98, 99, 100, 103, 110, 111, 114, 115, 116, 117, 118, 119, 120, 131, 149, 151, 161, 171.

haṭhayoga 171.

Hiraṇyagarbha 44, 149.

Hod 172.

Īśvara 44, 69, 85, 112, 113.

Jesus 15, 77, 78, 120, 124, 148, 172.

jīva 99, 101.

jīvanmukta 65, 129.

jīvātmā 134, 135, 140, 141, 142, 144, 149, 159, 161.

jīvātman 69.

Judaism 79.

kāma 140, 143, 173.

karma 55, 70, 145, 175.

Knowledge 11, 12, 13, 14, 21, 26, 37, 53, 60, 61, 70, 71, 85, 86, 93, 94, 96, 121, 145.

Lesser Mysteries 167. See also Mysteries.

Lesser *Opus* 167. See also *Opus*.

Liberated 65, 66, 67, 68 122, 129, 143.

līlā 14, 105, 106.

Logos 117, 118, 120.

manas 14, 60, 69, 85, 87, 137, 139, 140, 142, 143, 156, 157, 159, 163, 169, 170, 171, 172, 173.

Māṇḍūkya Upaniṣad 53, 58, 64.

manomaya 140.

materia prima 136, 166, 171.

māyā 12, 28, 32, 33, 35, 36, 59, 64, 65, 66, 67, 68, 69, 74, 76, 124, 142, 166, 176.

Meditation 83, 103, 169, 170, 171, 172.

Metempsychosis 21.

Musician 117, 118, 119.

Mysteries 164, 167.
  Egyptian Mysteries 164.
  Greater Mysteries 167.
  Lesser Mysteries 167.
nirguṇa Brahman 113. See also
  Brahman.
Nirmāṇakāya 148.
nirvāṇa 122, 124, 175.
Non-duality 11, 64.
noûs 117.
One-without-a-second 28, 64, 67.
Opus 167.
  Greater *Opus* 167.
  Lesser *Opus* 167.
Orphism 48, 151.
Pax profunda 13, 45, 66, 128.
Philosophy of Being 12, 38, 43,
  44, 45, 46, 47, 49, 51, 52,
  132.
Plato 83, 116, 149, 174.
Platonism 48.
post mortem 16, 155, 163.
prājña 140, 146.
prakṛti 101, 149, 156, 166.
prāṇa 68, 136, 137, 138, 139, 140,
  163.
pratyaya 170.
premayoga 78.
puruṣa 101, 166.
Pythagoras 115.

Qabbālāh 48, 172.
quinta essentia 138.
Ramana 67.
Ramana Maharsi 66.
Ratnasaṁbhava 148.
Reality 11, 15, 28, 29, 31, 32, 35,
  38, 39, 51, 56, 58, 65, 66, 67,
  68, 69, 73, 78, 79, 82, 85, 91,
  94, 101, 104, 112, 121, 132,
  138, 140, 156, 161.
Realization 16, 36, 44, 48, 55, 60,
  68, 82, 84, 85, 86, 115, 119,
  141, 145, 146, 158, 165, 166,
  169.
rūpa 144, 146, 150, 152.
sādhanā 55, 56, 59, 83, 84, 93,
  100, 121, 126, 141.
saguṇa Brahman 113. See also
  Brahman.
śakti 149.
samādhi 53, 146.
Saṁbhogakāya 148, 149, 150, 152,
  153.
Sāṁkhya 63, 166.
saṁsāra 16, 41, 122, 125, 148.
saṁskāra 94, 144, 153, 154.
Śaṅkara 15, 40, 60, 64, 66, 83,
  120, 134, 146, 155.
sat-cit-ānanda 78.
sattva 87, 139, 157, 161.
savikalpa samādhi 146.
Self 17, 47, 56, 94, 128, 153.

Sense of ego 154, 155, 158, 161, 170.

Sidpa Bardo 153. See also *Bardo*.

Śiva 146.

Social orders 46, 53, 120.

solve et coagula 138, 165, 170, 171.

Soul 21, 75, 85, 101, 110, 111, 112, 132, 141, 142, 145, 160.

Fall of the soul 75.

Subconsciousness 152.

Sufism 63.

Svabhāvikakāya 153.

taijasa 140, 144, 146, 148.

tapas 56.

Tat tvam asi 83.

Tradition 16, 49, 60, 63, 66, 67, 75, 89, 119, 125, 151, 166.

Turīya 53, 153.

Upaniṣad 14, 53, 58, 64, 86, 89, 152.

vāsanā 96, 153.

Veda 60, 68, 69.

Vedānta 30, 44, 48, 76, 83, 140, 142, 145, 153. See also *Advaita*.

Vibrating Life 107.

   Inner hearing 108, 111, 114, 116.

   Sound 29, 107, 109, 110, 112, 113, 114, 116, 117, 120, 172.

Tonal quality 107, 112, 117, 119.

Vibration 99, 107, 110, 111, 113, 117, 120, 134, 174.

vidyā 123.

vijñānamaya 140.

viśva 140.

Vivekacūḍāmaṇi 60.

yoga 63, 78, 84, 87, 121, 126, 158, 159, 169.

yogi 121, 136, 137, 138, 164.

yuga 52, 53.

   kaliyuga 53, 56.

   satyayuga 53, 56.

Zen 87.

RAPHAEL
Unity of Tradition

Having attained a synthesis of Knowledge (with which eclecticism or syncretism are not to be confused), Raphael aims at "presenting" the Universal Tradition in its many Eastern and Western expressions. He has spent a substantial number of years writing and publishing books on spiritual experience and his works include commentaries on the *Qabbālāh*, Hermeticism and Alchemy. He has also commented on and compared the Orphic Tradition with the works of Plato, Parmenides and Plotinus. Furthermore, Raphael is the author of several books on the pathway of non-duality (*Advaita*), and he has translated from the original Sanskrit, and offered commentaries on, a number of key Vedantic texts.

With reference to Platonism, Raphael has highlighted the fact that, if we were to draw a parallel between Śaṅkara's *Advaita Vedānta* and a Traditional Western Philosophical Vision, we could refer to the Vision presented by Plato. Drawing such a parallel does not imply a search for reciprocal influences, but rather it points to something of paramount importance: a sole Truth is inherent in the doctrines and teachings of several great thinkers, who although far apart in time and space, have reached similar and in some cases even identical conclusions.

One notices how Raphael writes in order to manifest and underscore the Unity of Tradition under a metaphysical perspective. This does not mean that he is in opposition to a dualistic perspective, or to the various religious faiths or "points of view."

A true embodied metaphysical Vision cannot be opposed to anything. What is important for Raphael is the unveiling, through living and being, of the level of Truth that one has been able to contemplate.

Written in the light of the Unity of Tradition, Raphael's works, calling on the reader's intuition, present precise points of correspondence between Eastern and Western Teachings. These points of reference are useful for those who want to approach a comparative doctrinal study and to enter the spirit of the Unity of Teaching.

For those who follow either an Eastern or a Western traditional line, these correspondences help us comprehend how the *Philosophia Perennis* (Universal Tradition), which has no history and has not been formulated by human minds as such, "comprehends universal truths that do not belong to any people or any age." It is merely for lack of "comprehension" or of "synthetic vision" that one particular Branch is considered the sole reliable one. Such a position only lead to opposition and fanaticism. What can degenerate the Doctrine is either a sentimental, fanatical devotion or a condescending intellectualism that is critical and sterile, dogmatic and separative.

In Raphael's words: "For those of us who aim at Realization, our task is to get to the essence of every Doctrine, because we know that just as Truth is one, so Tradition is one, even if, just like Truth, it may be viewed from a plurality of apparently different points of view. We must abandon all disquisitions concerning the phenomenal process of becoming and move onto the plane of Being. In other words, we must have a Philosophy of Being as the foundation of our search and of our realization."[1]

Raphael interprets spiritual practice as a "Path of Fire." Here is what he writes: "...The 'Path of Fire' is the pathway each

---

[1] See Raphael, *Tat tvam asi (That thou art): The Path of Fire according to the Asparśavāda* (New York: Aurea Vidyā, 2002).

disciple follows in all branches of Tradition; it is the Way of Return. Therefore, it is not the particular teaching of an individual or a path parallel to the one and only Main Road... After all, every disciple follows his own 'Path of Fire,' no matter which Branch of Tradition he belongs to."

In Raphael's view, what is important is to express through living and being the truth that one has been able to contemplate. Thus, for each being, one's expression of thought and action must be coherent and in agreement with one's own specific *dharma*.

After more than forty years of teaching, both oral and written, Raphael is now dedicating himself only to those people who, according to the expression of St. Paul, want to be "doers" rather than "sayers."

Raphael is connected with the *maṭha* founded by *Śrī Ādi* Śaṅkara at Śṛṅgeri, as well as with the *maṭha* at Kāñcīpuram and the Ramana Maharsi Āśram at Tiruvannamalai.

Founder of the Āśram Vidyā Order, Raphael now dedicates himself entirely to spiritual practice. He lives in a hermitage connected to the *āśram* and devotes himself completely to a vow of silence.

* * *

May Raphael's Consciousness, expression of Unity of Tradition, guide and illumine along this Opus all those who donate their *mens informalis* (non-formal mind) to the attainment of the highest known Realization.

PUBLICATIONS

Books by Raphael
published in English

At the Source of Life, *Questions and Answers Concerning the*
Ultimate Reality
Aurea Vidyā, New York

Beyond the illusion of the ego, *Synthesis of a Realizative Process*
Aurea Vidyā, New York

Essence and purpose of Yoga, *The Initiatory Pathways to the*
Transcendent
Element Books, Shaftesbury, U.K.

Initiation into the Philosophy of Plato
Aurea Vidyā, New York

Orphism and the Initiatory Tradition
Aurea Vidyā, New York

The Pathway of Fire according to the Qabbālāh,'Ehjeh 'Ašer
'Ehjeh (I am What I am)
Aurea Vidyā, New York

The Pathway of Non-duality, *Advaitavāda*
Motilal Banarsidass, New Delhi

The Science of Love, From the desire of the senses to the Intellect of Love
Aurea Vidyā, New York

Tat tvam asi, That thou art, The Path of Fire According to the *Asparśavāda*
Aurea Vidyā, New York

The Threefold Pathway of Fire, Thoughts that Vibrate
Aurea Vidyā, New York

Traditional Classics
in English

Śaṅkara, *Ātmabodha**, Self-knowledge
Aurea Vidyā, New York

Bhagavadgītā*, The Celestial Song
Aurea Vidyā, New York

Drigdriśyaviveka*, Discernment between Ātman and Non-Ātman.
Aurea Vidyā, New York

Gauḍapāda, *Māṇḍūkyakārikā**, The Metaphysical Path of Vedānta
Aurea Vidyā, New York

Parmenides, *On the Order of Nature***, Περί φύσεως, For a Philosophical Ascesis.

Patañjali, *The Regal Way to Realization** (*Yogadarśana*)
Aurea Vidyā, New York

Śaṅkara, *Vivekacūḍāmaṇi**, The Crest Jewel of Discernment
Aurea Vidyā, New York

Forthcoming Publications
in English

Śaṅkara, **Aparokṣānubhūti***, *Self-realization*

Bādarāyaṇa, **Brahmasūtra***

Five Upaniṣads*, *Īśa, Kaivalya, Sarvasāra, Amṛtabindu, Atharvaśira*

Raphael, **The Philosophers' Fire**

Raphael, **Which Democracy**, *References for a Good Government*

* Translated from the Sanskrit, and Commented, by Raphael
** Edited and Commented by Raphael

Aurea Vidyā is the Publishing House of the Parmenides Traditional Philosophy Foundation, a Not-for-Profit Organization whose purpose is to make Perennial Philosophy accessible.

The Foundation goes about its purpose in a number of ways: by publishing and distributing Traditional Philosophy texts with Aurea Vidyā, by offering individual and group encounters and by providing a Reading Room and daily Meditations at its Center.

* * *

Those readers who have an interest in Traditional Philosophy are welcome to contact the Foundation at: parmenides.foundation@earthlink.net.